to Mark, Grant, John, and Louie

PSYCHOLOGY OF COACHING

Thomas A. Tutko

Professor of Psychology
San Jose State College, California

Jack W. Richards

Head Basketball Coach
Gavilan College; Gilroy, California

PSYCHOLOGY
OF COACHING

Allyn and Bacon, Inc.
Boston · London · Sydney · Toronto

ISBN: 0-205-02904-3

Tenth printing ... September, 1976

CONTENTS

PREFACE

The strides made in athletics during the last twenty years have been enormous. Improvements in the techniques of play through better coaching, more efficient equipment, and superior physical conditioning methods have led to highly successful individual and team play. Coaching, at least from a technical standpoint, has become a very exact science, with few unknowns left. The modern coach is extremely well-versed in strategy; he is keenly aware of the values to be derived from weight training and proper nutrition; he knows how to protect his players and get the greatest efficiency from them through the use of various forms of new equipment.

He is also faced with coaching problems different from those of the past few decades. One of these is the personalities of the athletes themselves. The value orientation of today's young people is somewhat different from that of the past. The youth are more perceptive, more questioning, and have a greater variety of interests and experiences. As a result, the coach must become more sensitive to certain aspects of interpersonal behavior and motivational psychology. The purpose of this book is to explore these factors which are increasingly troubling to today's coach.

One basic assumption of this book is that individuals

are in athletics because they want to be, because they are getting something out of participation. Success, therefore, will help them further whatever goals they have in mind. These goals are more apt to be realized if the individual is handled in a personalized rather than a mechanical manner. Moreover, successful participation in athletics can set the pattern for responding to situations that occur later in life. Thus, athletics may be making a long-range contribution to individual development.

This book attempts to provide the coach with a practical guide for helping athletes to help themselves. It does not deal with the development of talent, but concentrates on the emotional and attitudinal aspects of athletic performance. In some instances the advice is based on psychological research; in others, where research is minimal or nonexistent, the suggestions are based on many hours of clinical observations and coaching experience. The science of the psychology of sport is relatively new and many questions remain unanswered. In time, the suggestions made in this book may be replaced or refined, as more accurate scientific knowledge becomes available. Hopefully, the coach will become more sensitive to individual needs and differences, not only in athletes but in teams as well, and will acquire in the process the flexibility to handle these differences.

Another objective of the authors is to put into non-technical language psychological principles which will help them deal with practical, everyday problems. Many coaches have been applying some of the concepts we deal with for a number of years. Other coaches feel that it takes too much time and effort for the eventual gains. A coach's attitudes will determine whether the procedures being advocated are to be given consideration.

We recommend that the coach select only those things with which he feels comfortable. As time progresses, he may feel at ease to explore additional areas. Too abrupt a change on the part of the coach may adversely affect some athletes already "adjusted" to a certain personality. A gradual incorporation of those ideas which the coach finds valuable is preferable. Designed to help in areas such as

Introduction to Coaching, The Psychology of Sport, Motivation in Athletics, Handling Individual Athletes, Psychology
of Coaching, Team Sports, etc., in fact, in any Physical
Education course where psychology plays a role, this book
attempts to furnish some basic guidelines to help stimulate
discussion and constructive action. In some circumstances,
giving copies of it to the entire team might help pinpoint
problem areas and enable coach and team to work toward
change most effectively.

An underlying premise is that developing the individual
athlete and team through greater communication, motivation, and individual attention is just as important as developing the game techniques, and that a coach who utilizes
these methods will get a great deal more from his athletes
than one who does not. To achieve maximum effectiveness
from each player and team, the coach must apply techniques
of motivation and communication unique to each situation.
The authors are deeply indebted to Dr. Bruce C. Ogilvie
for his many hours of discussion as well as encouragement
and continued support. Without his efforts the book would
not have reached fruition. It is hoped that this book, by
presenting information about a neglected area of athletics,
will enable the coach to develop a more dynamic and effective philosophy of coaching.

PSYCHOLOGY OF COACHING

chapter **1**

PHILOSOPHY OF COACHING

Sports have become a very vital part of our cultural heritage. Most Americans, either as active participants or as fans, view athletics with considerable interest. Participation in athletics is considered by many as an important part of the process of maturation—a kind of trial period during which the person develops character and learns to handle stress. There may be, in fact, no greater test of a person's character than to be placed in situations of stress like those found in athletics. The average individual does his work in private or unhampered by close, constant scrutiny; the athlete is required to exhibit his wares before his peers, as well as before the viewing audience, and few things can cause more anxiety in the human condition. It is as though he were constantly being evaluated. One small or minor mistake is in the open for a great number of others to view. The athlete feels as if he is under the powerful lens of a microscope. His every move is magnified. How he handles his athletic performance gives some indication of how he will handle other aspects of his life.

Athletics, then, may be seen as a kind of miniature model of life. If the person is outstanding in athletic competition, there is a high probability of his doing well in other areas. By "doing well" we do not mean to suggest that it is only his performance which serves as the measure of his potential success. "Doing well" also means his ability as a person to function with a high level of integrity and emotional maturity.

Many believe that athletics, for the most part, offers inherently beneficial values to the participant. There is wide acceptance of the theory that athletic participation has a considerably positive influence on the player with regard to responsibility, fair play, cooperation, concern for others, leadership, respect for authority, good citizenship, loyalty, and tolerance.

A few people are of the opinion that the athletic world represents a continuation of kid's games or child's play. Some feel that it represents a displacement of energy—that is, an opportunity for the participant to work out on the athletic field those things he cannot handle in other situations. Others even advocate the belief that athletic participation is a manifestation of psychopathology.

Although athletic participation may be regarded as child's play or displacement, it represents far more. When compared with other activities and occupations, it is an equally legitimate form of endeavor requiring highly developed talents and very delicate skills. There *is* evidence to indicate that if a person is disturbed or suffering from a number of personal problems, this will show up on the athletic field just as much, if not more so, than in everyday life, *but* athletics can hardly be seen as a substitute for, or as a release from, these problems. It is realistic to expect healthy or unhealthy personality traits to appear as an individual continues to perform. The person who blows his top and gets into fights on the field is probably going to do the same thing off the field, just as a hard worker on the field will be a hard worker off the field.

Seen in its finest and most realistic sense, athletic participation enables a man to learn discipline and to meet the challenge of facing other individuals mentally, physically, and emotionally.

THE COACH'S ATTITUDE

The coach is given the awesome and often thankless task of taking a relative neophyte and helping him develop into an individual possessing special talents and skills. The coach has the job of helping the athlete develop his talent to its fullest potential. This includes developing not only the athlete's innate physical attributes, but also his attitudinal, motivational, and psychological traits. Physical talent and mental attitude are both a part of performance, and if the coach develops one but not the other, he is not meeting his full coaching responsibility. In order to do this, the coach must have some understanding of his personal attitudes toward his job. He must develop a philosophy for coaching and handling his athletes effectively. This is not as easy to do as it may seem. It is not common for coaches to explore their personal philosophy. Moreover, it is uncommon for many coaches to develop a philosophy until they have had many years of experience; even then it may develop in a haphazard manner. To develop his philosophy, the coach must consider some of the more salient aspects of his sport and consider whether his approach toward these will have a positive or negative effect on his athletes.

Competition and Winning

The coach is charged with responsibilities beyond those of producing a winning team. Guiding and developing youth during the most critical years of physical, mental, and emotional development is one of his most important duties. The coach, perhaps more than any other school official, is in an excellent position to do this. For other faculty members, it is difficult to achieve the same degree of fellowship and natural intimacy that the coach enjoys with the students.

The coach's philosophy of coaching must of necessity be closely related to his philosophy of life. Winning games has too long been the yardstick for measuring coaching

success. This is not to say that the *will to win* is not important. It is very much a part of the *total* development of an
athlete, but of considerably greater importance to the coach,
as professional educator, should be the development of the
person.

The coach must understand how he can best motivate
the individual athlete, because within each athlete is the
potential to be successful. It is the coach's handling that will
enable each athlete to reach his full potential. The willingness of the coach to put in the time and the effort required
to produce the winning qualities is the basis of good coaching. Winning should be defined, by those who consider the
welfare of the individual athlete, as every player working
to his full potential. This does not necessarily mean that the
team in which each member fully participates will win a
championship every year. It does mean that they will quite
likely enjoy considerable athletic success. More importantly,
they will create habits and characteristics that will have
lasting value outside the sports environment. For a coach
to produce lasting values requires far more than just teaching the fundamentals of some particular form of athletics.
It means the coach must deal with each athlete as an individual; he must know the person he is teaching as well as
he knows how to teach the various techniques; and he must
realize how best to employ the talent of each athlete.

There are several ways to produce teams that will win
games. Some coaches put great effort into achieving quick
results, while others work slowly and steadily toward more
permanent goals. With the former, it may be a case of a
championship one year and the cellar the next. This is
often the case when a team is built around the outstanding
talent of one athlete. If he fails to produce, or when he
graduates, the entire attitude and philosophy of the coach
and the team change. There is little consistency. Although
the team that strives steadily toward permanent goals may
not be on top all the time, they will not fall from top to bottom. This approach requires more time, patience, and understanding with the individual players, but the results
are more solid and long-lasting. The truly great sports

dynasties were built with great care to produce men who thought, felt, and acted like winners.

Approaching the Athlete

Most coaches feel it is necessary to adjust to the *talent* available. They are quite willing to work to overcome physical shortcomings, but they are reluctant to adjust to the different *personality types* if it means changing an established approach. Most coaches can see the value of adjusting to the talent, but there is just as much advantage in adjusting to the different personality types. All too often coaches do not take the time to become acquainted with their athletes, since they do not see this as a major part of athletic success. Moreover, coaches are very rarely taught how to handle interpersonal behavior, nor are they instructed in team interaction or motivation. Most coaches must rely upon a philosophy that has taken years of coaching to develop, or they simply imitate the coaches who have trained them. Usually in these cases, the philosophies do not include motivational or psychological techniques for handling the athletes as individuals.

Some coaches actually look down on their athletes or regard them as naive and in need of being governed totally. The coach exercises complete control over them. The better philosophy suggests that the players are individuals in their own right, and, to bring out potential talent, they need to be understood and handled in terms of their own needs. The first philosophy may produce a winning team, but it will also eliminate a lot of potentially productive athletes. The latter will produce a greater number of winners, because it allows for the development of several different personality types by using as the frame of reference the individual player rather than the coach.

The coach's attitude toward talent also depends upon an assessment of his own ability. A coach may see a person who is not using his talent and become irate. Some coaches feel it is their religious duty to develop talent whether or not the athlete desires it. Actually it is the individual's option to develop or not develop his talent. The coach can only provide him with the opportunity. For example, coaches who have only had a minimal talent are often very judgmental about a talented athlete who decides to abandon the sport. The coach, in this case, may be working out his own desires vicariously.

If a coach were given the opportunity to go out on the field and select from the talent the particular personality type that fits his concept of a winner, the athlete would probably be a champion. Ordinarily, the coach is not in that position. He does not have the luxury of selecting players who are totally desirable or perfect, as he sees the situation. The players must adjust to the coach, of course, but it is a reciprocal agreement. The coach must also adjust to some degree to be able to understand the players. We are speaking now of the coach's style and not his personality. The coach cannot be asked to change his personality, but he can become aware of the fact that other approaches are equally valid and acceptable. Certain types of handling will account for the loss of some players. By the same token, the same handling techniques may be responsible for the realization of the full potential of another athlete.

A fair question to be asked of all coaches is, "How many talented athletes have you lost along the way because of a difference in personality?" or "Once you have selected a team, do you try to force every player to exhibit certain behaviors, or do you take what the individual has and use it to the athlete's best advantage?"

Special traits exhibited by some players will be viewed by certain coaches as negative. These coaches not only cannot use the trait to help the player become a winner, but also may actually *lose* the player because of a personal prejudice against the trait. For example, a coach may be totally unable to work with a stubborn athlete, while another finds it impossible to deal with a withdrawn person. A sensitive athlete may be intolerable to one coach, while another coach dislikes a showoff. If the coach can discern any kind of consistent pattern in the type of person he is losing, or the traits that annoy him, it may well be that it is the coach's personal problem. He may, of course, choose to continue to lose that type of player, but he must understand that a wealth of talent may be escaping him. For example, a coach has strong feelings against exhibitionists, and the outstanding characteristic exhibited by one of his more talented players is that very trait. The coach may either ridicule him or get angry with him for seeking the spotlight and thus lose him. On the other hand, he may understand the player's need and set specific guidelines for him to follow in his quest to achieve success—score more points, get more rebounds, or make more tackles. When the player produces, the coach provides what is, for the player, a big need and a major motivation. The team rules should provide controls to prevent the individual player's trait from becoming a negative force.

Motivating the Athlete

Another important philosophical issue to be examined by the coach is whether to motivate positively or negatively. A great deal of the philosophy of coaching is a philosophy of how to motivate. Does the coach believe in punishing when the player does wrong, or does he believe in complimenting when he does right? Or does he use a combination?

The coach must be aware of the effect punishment (negative reinforcement) will have on the player. With punishment, fear will emerge. The source of the fear may become hated. Since fear has the tendency to cause people to band together if they have the same fear in common, some teams become very close, because they are terrified of the coach. If he uses fear and treats everybody equally, it is likely that the team will feel a sense of satisfaction at having met the coach's rigid expectations. Providing the team wins by using this approach, fear does have some rewarding qualities.

Teams who are punished but win hold together as long as they are winning. Teams who are punished a great deal but lose usually fall apart. On some teams there is often a lot of subtle rebelling, and the players form cliques. The fear approach cannot be sustained over a long period of time unless there are some notable rewards. A team conditioned to win as a result of fright eventually must have fear to win. The minute the fear is eliminated, they stop producing. For example, if a team goes from a fear-producing, punitive coach to a very easy-going coach, the players may produce initially, but since the fear is not there to sustain them as it has been in the past the team will fall apart. They simply do not have the same fear-producing stimuli, and they have to re-group to adjust to the new coach. Anything less than punishment is non-motivational for them. The coach can almost plan on a failure if he uses fear exclusively, treats his players unequally, and does not have sufficient initial success.

If complimentary means (positive reinforcement) are used, the person's feelings about himself are enhanced, and a much longer-lasting closeness and identification with other players is developed. The individual athletes are more apt also to produce when the agent of the reinforcement is absent. In essence, the coach gets more from the athlete in the long run by supporting him than he would by punishing him. If the coach is totally comlimentary, not receiving a compliment may be a form of punishment. By omission the player is punished. It may sound as though we suggest that the only way to handle an athlete is to compliment him. This is not so. The nature of sport is such that a certain amount of toughness, aggression, and assertiveness is necessary, and limits have to be set and firmly adhered to by the coach.

Perhaps most coaches use a combination of positive and negative reinforcement. That is, they punish errors, but compliment effective or successful play. Even though this may be the case, some coaches tend to punish more than they reward, while others reward more than they punish. If asked, coaches are apt to report that they use a combination of both, simply because they have no means of checking the frequency with which they use either. Some coaches *feel* they use a combination, but actually do not *openly express* their positive feelings. They do not compliment the athlete because "If the athlete has done well, he doesn't need a compliment—he knows he has done well." They believe that it is unnecessary to compliment the obvious. The athlete, however, has no way of knowing what the coach is thinking. He is only aware of the coach's criticism.

It is important that the combination be of equal intensity. It is quite likely that the negative comment will far outweigh the positive comment in the mind of the athlete, anyway, but the coach sometimes tends to equate a somewhat off-handed comment like "Nice game!" with a prolonged and forceful humiliation of the athlete before his peer group. Few players have been destroyed by compliments, while many have been driven from further competition by a coach's criticisms.

Losing

Each coach has an attitude toward losing and losers. If the coach sees a loser as weak, inadequate, and someone to be made fun of, he not only loses the respect of the player, but he also forces the player to win, if possible, through a sense of fear. If a loser is seen as someone who tried his best and did not quite make it, instead of all the other negative connotations usually associated with losing, respect is still present, and the player may be allowed to pursue relevant goals without undue pressure.

Each coach must explore his own attitude toward losing. The toughest aspect of coaching is not to learn how to handle winning, but how to handle losing, particularly if the coach knows he had the talent and still did not make them produce. Some coaches feel that if they are very tough on athletes, they are absolved of the blame for lack of success. A coach may say, "Well, I did my best. I did everything I could. I drove them as hard as I could." The coach feels if he is tough, others will think he has done his best. The coach might be much more successful if he allowed understanding to replace toughness. Sensitivity and toughness do not need to be in opposition.

Most athletes who participate have some question, however slight, about an aspect of their ability. Few individuals have complete self-confidence. The coach who looks upon losing and losers with contempt threatens that part in the athlete that does not possess full confidence. Where support and encouragement may help the athlete face and overcome that sensitive area, a coach who threatens and humiliates only generates more pain and fear in the athlete so that he may never be able to develop fully and overcome his weakness. Moreover, the athlete is apt to hide his weakness as much as possible from a punishing coach, thus preventing the athlete from further growth. For example, a baseball player who has difficulty with ground balls may be so frightened of being humiliated by the coach if he misses a ground ball that his fear may begin to interfere with other aspects of his game. His batting may be affected, or he may concentrate on batting rather than fielding in order to avoid embarrassment on the field. On the other hand, if he felt supported by the coach, he would want to overcome that weakness in his game.

THE RESPECTED COACH

Although most coaches would feel it a tribute to be liked by their players, they probably would prefer to be respected. It is often difficult for the coach to know if he is being respected. Respect is likely to take an indirect rather than a direct form. It is often manifested as the absence of adverse behavior or team problems. For example, an athlete or team that respects the coach usually has a minimum number of team rules broken. The athletes feel it is their responsibility to show their respect by following, rather than violating, team regulations. There is often less absenteeism, fewer cliques, less griping, and fewer signs of dissension on a team where the coach is respected. One clear sign of respect is that there is little, if any, undercutting of the coach and few snide or derogatory remarks. In fact, if they do occur, other team members are quick to remind the athlete making the remark that he is out of line.

The coach may be a former athlete and, in a way, is still participating in the sport, but in a very unique manner.

The coach must remember that he is no longer an active
member of the game. For some coaches it is hard to make
that adjustment. They are still vicariously in the action and
often unable to remove themselves from the old, active role.
There is confusion as to who they are and what they are
doing. To gain the respect of his team, the coach must realize
that he participates, *but* in a very unique way.

The coach can never be sure about the amount or degree
of respect each individual athlete holds for him. The coach
can only be sure of his behavior in attempting to gain and
maintain respect. Although there may be numerous reasons
why players respect the coach, there are several which are
apt to bring about a greater amount of respect than others.

1 Knowledge of the Sport

Each player would like to believe the coach is an expert and
that he has more knowledge about the game than any other
person on the team. The athletes would like to have the security of knowing that if they get into a difficult spot, the
coach will be able to come up with a solution.

2 Individual Concern

Each athlete would like to believe that the coach is interested in him as an individual, that the coach is concerned
about the welfare of the athlete, and that the coach views
him as more than just a human being with athletic talent.
Each athlete would like to believe he is recognized as a person and not as something to be used as a pawn in a game.
Resentment is often felt by an athlete who believes he is
only a cog in a wheel.

3 Fairness

Each athlete would like to feel he will be given an equal
opportunity to demonstrate his talent and that he will not
be ignored if his performance is not up to par. To be treated
unfairly or to have the coach show favoritism is often one of
the greatest reasons for disrespect. The athlete who feels

he is giving his all while the coach is holding back and the athlete who feels left out can hardly perform to full capacity for the coach.

4 Coach as an Example

Athletes would like to know that the coach adheres to the rules and regulations just as well as the players. This does not mean that the coach should participate in the actual playing or should go through the exercises; it does mean that if the players are asked to maintain a bed check, the coach should be willing to adhere to the same kind of rule, at least to a reasonable degree. The coach who violates his own rules creates a great amount of disrespect. As an example, a coach who demands that the players maintain a certain weight during the season, yet is himself obese does not command the greatest respect. He should demonstrate behavior which will assure the team that he, too, is willing to make sacrifices in an effort to become successful. Obviously the coach should have certain privileges, but to flaunt them or use them contrary to the demands of the team brings disrespect.

5 Maturity

The players look up to the coach as a symbol of maturity. He is expected to provide a model for them to follow. If he responds in an infantile fashion, he will lose the respect of his players. To make fun of someone, even if it is the opponent, to take advantage of someone who is helpless or less fortunate, or to cheat are all ways in which the coach can lose the respect of his players. This disrespect eventually manifests itself in a poorer performance by the team.

THE SCOPE OF ATHLETICS

There are many different philosophies inherent in sports activity representing the many different philosophies of life.

The scope of athletic participation is such that it takes into consideration almost all kinds of talent and personalities— everything from the total isolation of marathon distance running to the pile of bodies at the line of scrimmage—and utilizes the full range of body types—thin, heavy, frail, muscular, tall, short, large, and small. An individual may be competing as a part of a complex and highly coordinated unit or he may be competing individually. Some athletes must command a full range of skills, while others are valued for their speciality—kicking field goals or defending goals, attacking passers or defending passers. Some aspects of competition require no contact whatsoever, while others place the athlete in great physical danger. Some challenges are very personal and others are totally impersonal.

In developing his own philosophy of coaching, the coach at one time or another must consider seriously each of the areas discussed in this chapter. A coach's philosophy must be ever-changing and dynamic. A coach whose philosophy remains unchanged fails to move with the times. In the final analysis, the coach must decide what is best for his players, his team, and himself.

chapter **2**

THE COACH AND HIS PERSONALITY

Just as individual differences exist among the members of a team, a variety of personality types can be identified in the coaching profession. Each person reacts differently to almost any given situation depending to a large extent on the nature of his personality.

A student, in his educational experience, has no closer contact with a teacher than he does with his coach. His close relationship with the coach over a period of months—the work, the agony, the disappointment, and the glory of success—produces an atmosphere in which the coach can become a truly influential builder of character and a molder of personality. It is essential, then, that the coach not only understand the individual differences which exist among the members of his squad, but also know his own personality. This can be a complex matter, because it is difficult for someone to be objective about himself. Most people tend either to overlook their shortcomings or to justify their position in one way or another.

The coach in a somewhat dictatorial position is prone to insist that the personality adjustment occur on the part of the athlete. As an "authority," the coach is sometime‾

reluctant to admit that success and the healthiest educational atmosphere for the participant may lie in the coach's ability to adjust.

Psychological insight can offer increased effectiveness in coaching. As a matter of fact, the degree of success a coach enjoys may be seriously diminished by his unwillingness to examine the mechanisms responsible for his attitudes and personality.

The following ideas provide a basis for the personality classifications to be discussed in this chapter and should be kept in mind when considering the coach's relationship to the individual athlete or to the team as a whole:

1. The coach has salient personality characteristics.
2. The coach's personality may shape the personality of the individual with whom he works. The younger the athlete, the higher the probability that this is true. As the athlete becomes more mature, this is less apt to be the case. Moreover, the closer and more frequent the contact between coach and athlete, the higher the probability that this will be true.
3. The coach's personality affects his philosophy of athletics and, in turn, reflects the type of team he produces.

In an attempt to illustrate how coaches with varied personalities produce a variety of player responses, we have placed coaches in five general categories: the hard-nose or authoritarian coach, the nice guy coach, the intense or driven coach, the easy-going coach, and the business-like coach. The advantages and disadvantages of each personality type in regard to coaching and handling the athlete are presented and discussed. We do not mean to suggest that all coaches will fall exclusively into any one category, nor do we imply that coaches fall into only the five categories we discuss. These are only the most predominant categories. Other categories may emerge in time, and some coaches defy classification, because they are totally unique in their approaches. There is no "ideal" coach, nor one who is completely effective. Success depends on a number of elements such as talent, technique, circumstances, the personality make-up of the team, and often just plain luck. Most coaches are constantly applying the trial and error method to come up with more effective means of handling their athletes. In our analysis, an overlapping of characteristics within each category is the rule rather than the exception, but a predominance of traits in one category points to certain tendencies and typical reactions.

I. THE "HARD-NOSED," AUTHORITARIAN COACH[1]

In all probability most readers will immediately recognize this type of coach. Most people have had contact with the hard-driving and energetic man who demands a certain response from his players and who constantly compels the athlete to strive to achieve well-formulated goals. Admiration for this man is likely to depend upon several factors: the degree of success he is able to achieve; the similarity of his goals and objectives to the athletes'; and his physical stature or his athletic prowess. As time passes it is also likely that appreciation of this man deepens and an experience with him comes to be regarded as beneficial, much as one looks back upon military service with a sense of nostalgia. This type of coach has certain limitations. For example, his judgment is not always perfect—in strict and stubborn adherence to his personal code he sometimes overlooks other possible solutions to individual or team problems. He tends to rely more upon exhortation and stimulation than on an analytical examination of the problem. His approach does, on occasion, produce an almost magical performance from the "keyed-up" performer, but without a sound basis in fundamental techniques or a careful analysis of the situation, the athlete is likely to experience his share of defeats and frustration.

---

1. A great deal of the work on authoritarianism has been summarized in the following: J. P. Kirscht and R. C. Dillehay, *Dimensions of Authoritarianism, A Review of Research and Theory* (Lexington: University of Kentucky Press, 1967).

This man is best remembered for the forms of "punishment" he devises to enforce his "hard-nose" policies. Players run laps, do push-ups, take early showers, or even find themselves pitted against him in a competitive situation when they do not live up to his standards.

We have devoted the greatest amount of time to this personality type because it has the largest number of coaches within its descriptive boundaries. It is also the type most often emulated by beginning coaches, and the type most generally seen by the public as successful, particularly in the area of contact sports.

Characteristics

1. *Believes strongly in discipline*   This man feels that success and accomplishment are achieved by strict devotion to stated goals. There is no excuse for indolence and no substitute for hard work. He "drives" his teams, often unmercifully, and expects nothing short of complete dedication on the part of each team member.

2. *Usually uses punitive measures to enforce rules*   In his effort to achieve complete dedication and an all-out effort from each player, the coach often resorts to forms of punishment which, when not carefully thought out, may result in ill feeling and bitter resentment on the part of the athlete who may feel that the coach has embarrassed him or judged him unfairly. One unkind word or gesture at the wrong moment may permanently alienate an athlete, particularly if he feels that he has been unjustly accused. This trait is generally associated with the "old school" of coaching which emphasizes toughness and severity in the handling of athletes. The coach is often unforgiving if someone should commit some act that he considers unfair to him.

3. *Rigid about schedules and plans*   It naturally follows that there should be a strong insistence by this coach that the athlete pay very close attention to details relating to even the most routine matters. The athlete who is not fully aware

of this fact may find the door locked to the gym if he is late, or the uniform removed from his locker if he is slovenly about its care, or that he is not allowed to make the trip if he was "horsing around" in a chalk talk, or that he is permanently dropped from the team if he breaks any of the training rules, or that he is left behind by the bus if he arrives a few minutes late. The list of examples could go on and on, but the point is that there is little flexibility to be found in the practices of the hard-nose coach off the field as well as on.

4. *Can be cruel and sadistic (often insulting)* When players fall short of the coach's expectations, the "weakness" is usually met with a sharp verbal barrage most generally in the presence of other team members. All members of the team are eligible for these caustic remarks and will probably feel his sharp criticism at some time during the season. Some players accept these barbs quite well and the effect is beneficial. Others of a more sensitive nature may be severely hurt by them and withdraw or react in anger. In these instances the coach may appear to be quite cruel, which he is if he has not carefully considered the nature of the individual he attacks. From another point of view, he may be considered extremely fair, because all the players are treated in the same manner, at least on the surface. He is apt to show favoritism in a very subtle way. For example, the quarterback does not go through the same severe training, or the coach will constantly select players he believes are the hard workers and will give them the lion's share of the credit. In many instances they are just his personal favorites. The favoritism he does show can hardly be detected.

Not usually a warm personality The hard-nose coach is most often withdrawn from his players. This distance is due to his continued refusal to accept anything but a perfect performance. The coach is reluctant to get too close to the player for fear that in some way the player will take advantage of his position and expect some sort of preferential treatment. It is a rare occasion when this coach praises the efforts of any player. A terse comment such as "Good game, Johnson!" may become quite important to the player and may represent the coach's highest form of acceptance.

6. *Very organized and well planned*   An important fact to keep in mind about this coach is that he is sincere and genuinely interested in doing a good job. He is extremely industrious and willing to spend as much time as necessary to achieve his goals. He does not like to waste time, and he hates any unnecessary and pointless effort. Practices, therefore, are usually well planned and there is seldom any inactivity or time unaccounted for.

7. *Does not like to get too close interpersonally*   Both the player and the coach find it difficult to relate socially. An "understanding gap" is very likely to exist, again because of the distance the coach likes to maintain between himself and the athlete.

8. *Often religious and moralistic*   It is to be expected that this man may have very high principles and actively support many fine causes. He may attend church regularly and espouse the most moral of all positions in his relationship with other human beings. A number of interesting reasons may be given for this position. As a dynamic, forceful, and sometimes ruthless man in his professional life, he searches for and finds in religious affiliation an escape from a form of guilt which he may unconsciously associate with his rather violent professional world. Also it is quite likely that he has been influenced at some point in his life by an individual or a situation that emphasized the need for a relentless and energetically forceful position to achieve the goal. It is also quite possible that the man learned through his athletic experience that personal initiative, and not timidity, led to respect and social acceptance by his peers.

9. *Often bigoted and prejudiced*   With a man who possesses so many preconceived notions about human achievement, it

is possible that he may classify racial and ethnic groups on the basis of limited experiences with individuals belonging to these groups. In his often frenzied attempt to fight time, he conveniently "pre-judges" people or anticipates certain responses, which opens up the possibility for reducing his potential for success. Sadly enough, his notions are reinforced regularly by selective observances and constant communication with other coaches who share his views.

10. *Prefers weaker people as assistant coaches* This is a "strong" man: strong willed, persuasive, and dominating. It is very unlikely that a similar personality type will be found on the same coaching staff, for the simple reason that a clash would probably result. Usually a "winning" combination of personality types is found on successful coaching staffs—a "hard-nose" paired with the "easy-going" or with the "nice-guy" type. The hard-nose coach serves as the real symbol of authority—the tyrant, if you will—who drives unmercifully, but who has difficulty identifying with the participant. The nice-guy or easy-going coach presents to the athlete a sympathetic outlet for his emotions—someone to whom he can relate when things are not going well or when he simply needs understanding. This situation is a "bad guy–good guy" balance. It is an emotionally healthy situation for most athletes who actually want to be driven, but who insist that they be understood during the process. Of course, great loyalty must exist on this kind of staff or open rebellion may result with the outcome being a victory for neither coach. Intelligent and perceptive coaches *balance* the staff for these reasons.

Uses threats to motivate In a sense the athlete who plays for the hard-nose coach feels threatened all the time. He must. For a variety of reasons, all athletes experience periods of mediocrity and difficulty. Feeling threatened makes these times doubly frightening. They are upsetting for personal reasons, but they are also disturbing because the player can expect a severe censure from the coach as he makes an effort to elicit the best possible effort from all team members. So the coach may motivate his athletes by external or obvious threats such as making them run more laps and do more pushups. He may also motivate on a psychological level by threatening the athlete with criticism and embarrassment. As stated earlier, many athletes respond magnificently to this kind of motivation and are actually driven to superior achivements, while others may succumb to its oppressiveness and either quit or have their performance level diminish markedly.

Advantages

1. *Disciplined club*   Usually the team is infected with the coach's intensity and devotion to a cause. The players may exhibit a certain rigidity in their approach to their goals. They may be obsessed with an objective and exhibit a strict disciplinary code of conduct. This atmosphere is conducive to a high degree of success if other factors are present. Most certainly if early success occurs and momentum is developed, an outstanding season is probable. Usually the team continues throughout the season in the same manner and with the same devotion. Most coaches strongly desire this situation where players have a sense of dedication and purpose. When the team "clicks," it is unbeatable.

2. *Usually aggressive and physically punishing team*   The team's intensity usually manifests itself in a high degree of aggressiveness. The players are confident, eager for competition, and spirited in the contest. They also tend to be slightly pugnacious which is in keeping with the toughness inculcated in them by their coach. They are very likely to annihilate a weaker team, but they may not always fare too well when they encounter a superior team. They intimidate their opponents and are sometimes famous (or infamous) for their callous destructiveness.

3. *Well-organized team*   Organization plays an important part in the success of any team. It means that they will probably

be prepared for most situations which arise. They have been well drilled and appreciate the power and pleasure which goes with mastery of fundamental situations. Phases of the game become routine through daily practice.

4. *Usually team in better physical condition than other teams* One of the first statements heard by a player who is handled by a hard-nose coach is "No one will beat us physically!" It *is* an area in which the coach can exert some measurable controls. If the athlete can survive the blistering conditioning program prepared and carried out by this coach, he does stand a better chance of survival in the rugged battle before him. There is no greater sense of satisfaction for an athlete than to know and feel that he is *really* in shape. Most athletes will admit that they have been in top physical condition only a few times in their entire careers. It is most likely to occur under the tutelage of the authoritarian coach.

5. *Good team spirit when winning* As was stated earlier, when this team has momentum they are extremely difficult to beat. They have outstanding enthusiasm, the spirit of comradeship is high, and an aura of optimism is evident. The most significant result of this confidence is its effect on other teams, which are overwhelmed by it.

Disadvantages

1. *Team prone to dissension when things go badly* It is foolish to say that anyone can be adequately prepared to accept adversity and defeat. We very rarely expect defeat in athletics, and only the most uninvolved immediately shrug it off without some effect or concern. The authoritarian's team does show a tendency to lose badly. The team members look for excuses or for others to blame for the failure. When firm convictions and confidence are shattered, it is difficult to rebound with the same degree of enthusiasm and desire. Introspection and intelligent analysis have not been encour-

aged in this atmosphere and so, without a substantial knowledge of all contributing factors, the players and coach are likely to grasp at straws in an attempt to explain the inadequacy.

2. *Sensitive athletes unable to handle such treatment and usually drop out* The more an athlete is made to feel like an individual and the greater the respect he receives from those about him, the more responsive he will be to the coach and the more apt he is to feel an important part of the team. In an atmosphere where punishment or fear of criticism exists, the more sensitive athlete may never be made to feel at all important, making it impossible for him to identify with the other team members or with the coach. If this occurs, it is very unlikely that he will be able to reach his potential as an athlete. This is less of a problem on the professional and college level where the coach can select the tougher-minded and less sensitive athlete. On a high school or junior high level, however, the coach must make the best use of players he has. He cannot be selective, so he must handle the sensitive, as well as the tough athletes.

3. *Coach often disliked or feared* It is easy to build up resentment against a person who represents authority if that authority uses punitive measures to enforce rules. If an athlete has built up resentment for the coach, he will find this emotion difficult to express openly, because it most certainly will bring some form of reprisal when it is observed, such as being dismissed from the team. Direct anger, therefore, is not possible and a more subtle means of acting out the resentment may be necessary. The team member may unconsciously undermine the coach's intentions by doing everything he can to have him fail. If this spreads to any degree throughout the team, serious dissension must result and little success or anything of lasting value can result from the experience.

4. *Team often driven and tense when unnecessary* Almost all athletes feel driven at some time during the season.

When fatigue sets in or when a team is under unusual stress, some external stimuli is needed to help them fight through difficult moments. Almost every competitor realizes this and expects it. What he does not expect is to be driven during times when he feels the need and the inclination to relax a bit and enjoy the fun of competition and membership on the team. If his reaction is markedly different from the coach's during these periods, conflict may occur. The situation may become extremely tense if both parties attempt to justify their position, and in doing so distort the image of the other person. This, again, can lead to anger, and distrust, and an impossible situation.

5. *Preparation "simple" in approaching a game with this type of team*   This team can be expected to follow a rigid and somewhat predictable game plan. They rarely rely on the element of surprise or on "razzle-dazzle" tactics. They are not prone to spontaneity. Their repertoire of plays is usually limited. The hard-nosed "bread-and-butter" approach is their answer to cleverness. Preparation by the opposing team, *from the point of view of what to expect*, is not very complex. Preparing them to *handle* that team is another matter!

THE "NICE-GUY" COACH

Characteristics of the "nice-guy" coach are nearly opposite from those of the hard-nose coach. The nice-guy coach is personable, well liked by others, flexible, and deeply concerned with the welfare of his players. This is not to say that the hard-nose coach may not be concerned also, but the expression of concern is more evident in the nice-guy coach. He commands respect for entirely different reasons than the authoritarian coach. He is popular, and he is sociable. His home is open to his players, and they are welcome in it. He sponsors activities, is directly involved in many ways with student affairs, and finds genuine pleasure in the association.

Characteristics

1. *Usually liked by a number of people*   Here is a man with whom most players can feel at ease. The depth of their relationship ranges all the way from a cheerful and relaxed gaiety in his presence on campus to very serious discussions of complex personal problems in his home. This quality can be important in terms of success, since players want to win for him as a form of reciprocity.

2. *Considerate of others*   The personal well being of each player is a major consideration with this coach. He is concerned with the individual's academic standing, his future college goals, and seeing to it that the player receives the greatest value from his athletic experience.

3. *Uses positive means to motivate athletes*   In keeping with the other characteristics, it naturally follows that the nice-guy is much more disposed to use positive methods of reinforcement then criticism and threats to achieve his ends. He is generous with his compliments and tactful in expressing his criticism. Outstanding efforts are recognized by this man and special awards are devised to reward the athlete.

4. *Very flexible in planning—sometimes chaotic*   The nice-guy sees the value of flexibility and makes allowances for deviations in the normal schedule of events. He is not insistent upon pursuing any one method or procedure, and his approach may change quite drastically within any given season. This slightly chaotic condition may lead to some confusion and frustration, and even doubt, on the part of his players as to his mastery of the fundamentals and his competency as a coach.

5. *Often experimental*   He remains open-minded and sees the value in other systems and styles of play. He is reluctant to adopt just one method and thus close his mind to other possibilities. It may be that he lacks experience in competitive

athletics. He may never have been thoroughly indoctrinated into any one system and is a bit unsure of himself. He may, on occasion, use gimmicks and be impressed by the success of other coaches to the extent that he actually imitates or adopts their approaches without careful analytical thought. A player may find that "last week's offense" has just been dumped and is being replaced with an entirely new attack.

Advantages

1. *Good team cohesiveness*   Players who are close to one another tend to play well together. Under the nice-guy coach, the players are more prone to develop a genuine feeling for one another. This is due, in part, to the absence of threat, but more importantly it is due to the prolonged and close personal involvement of players and coach. A healthy mutual respect and admiration results. The word "team," in the true sense of the word, takes on a real meaning.

2. *Athletes produce beyond that expected of them*   Evidence indicates that these players are capable of great success—success, that is, beyond a point expected of them. This is a bit misleading. Athletes who perform for a hard-nose coach never can satisfy and subsequently never reach the level expected of them. The other, less threatened athlete builds on continual success. Each level of accomplishment is recognized and rewarded and becomes a substantial stepping stone to the next.

3. *Team usually relaxed*   Genuine enjoyment of an activity occurs in greater depth on this team. The *fun* of competition is not interfered with by the stress that accompanies it. The players eagerly look forward to practices, rather than dread them. It is probably true that there is harmony on this team and many strong friendships. Winning is important, but it is not necessarily a life and death matter. Defeats are "taken in stride" a little better and periods of depression are shorter and less severe. The team rarely is punished for doing poorly.

4. *Problem athletes handled more effectively* Because the members of this team are treated as individuals and because sincere concern is shown for their welfare, the person who is suffering some form of anxiety will be far less likely to withdraw or drop out altogether. The coach is simply more aware of the player's needs and motivations. He works around the problems. He avoids any action which might intensify the difficulty. He uses his knowledge of the situation to help eliminate the stress, as best he can. As a result, greater athletic success can be achieved and maintained.

Disadvantages

1. *Coach often seen as weak* Under the nice-guy coach, it is to be expected that some players will see, in the absence of force, an opportunity to get away with as much as possible. It is an easy situation to take advantage of, if the athlete is so inclined. In general, many people will view this man as weak, indecisive, and incompetent because of his flexibility and somewhat unorthodox methods. This is especially true if the team is having a bad season. It is very easy to blame the coach, because he probably blames himself already.

2. *"Con men" not handled well* The con man shows respect for superior power only. The most effective coach for handling the con man is one who can be superior to him. The coach must consistently assert power and meet every test with force that the con man can present.

3. *May lose socially inhibited athletes* The coach who is a nice-guy may frighten socially inhibited athletes. If he tries to become acquainted with them, they will withdraw. This is particularly true of athletes who have had a history of negative relationships with authority figures. The athlete may feel the coach is simply using him and will fail to interact. Because most athletes are apt to respond to the nice-guy, he will be puzzled by the athlete who withdraws. Any

attempts to get better acquainted only intensifies the situation. The coach may lose such an athlete altogether. This is particularly true of athletes whose backgrounds show extreme hardship with parents. It is important for the coach to know the interaction of each athlete with his parents, especially the athlete's father.

INTENSE OR "DRIVEN" COACH

The intense coach is similar in many ways to the hard-nose coach. The intense coach exhibits many of the traits already described in the section on the authoritarian and may even be considered as a sub-type. He is similar in his emphasis on discipline, in his strength of will, and in his aggressiveness. However, there are several marked differences. The basic differences are that he is less punitive and more emotional. He rather seriously lacks composure, which is in contrast to the tough, but comparatively quiet, authoritarian.

Characteristics

Frequently worried   Here is the guy who really gets the ulcers. He is never content. He always feels that something is undone, and he is convinced that this will be the cause of his defeat in the upcoming game. Details drive him crazy. He is constantly plagued by his own guilt over not having covered some aspect of the scouting report, not emphasizing a phase of the attack thoroughly enough, the way he handled last night's practice, etc.

Overemphasizes or dramatizes situations   This is the towel-chewer, the screamer, the umpire-baiter, the truly involved "do-or-die" competitor. In an impassioned half time speech, he may implore the players to win for the honor of the school, or get very angry at the team and accuse them of disloyalty because they were not listening in a chalk talk, or he may re-play the game a hundred times while trying to go to sleep at night. Most of the time the man is sincere. Competitive athletics is the most important thing in the world to him.

3. *Takes things personally* This man is so directly involved that everything is personal. The official is "out to get him"; players who do not live up to his standards are deliberately trying to undermine his efforts; the loss last week was due to his own lack of emphasis on defense.

4. *Spends endless hours on materials* Charts, graphs, statistics, and signs all give evidence of this coach's concern with details. If possible, he will leave nothing to chance, employing every means he can think of to control the variables. His scouting is thorough, and the information is given to his players in numerous handout sheets. The locker room is probably filled with slogans and all kinds of signs intended to provide an additional stimulus to the players.

5. *Always has complete knowledge of the game* This man is very well informed. He spends a great deal of time studying other teams, other systems of play, and other methods of instruction. He talks with other coaches, is present at as many practices and games of other teams as time will allow, and is knowledgeable about a remarkable number of players on a variety of levels.

6. *Always pushing himself—never satisfied with his accomplishments* The intense coach is plagued by a desire for perfection. He is never *really* happy with a game or his team's performance, because he can see only the mistakes that need correcting. He has an exact picture of what he wants and is displeased with anything less.

7. *Motivates players by his example* This man usually will not ask his players to do anything that he is not willing to do himself. He is probably the most involved person on the team. In the first place, he spends *much* more time with the

game than anyone else. He gets more excited and takes losses
very hard. Players do not necessarily feel driven *by* him;
it is more as though they are driven to *keep up with* him.
His presence is a constant stimulus and players find that
they get caught up in this frenzied pace. It is nearly impossible to be passive or unconcerned.

Advantages

1. *Team usually "up" for a contest*   Apathy is not a problem
with this team. Players are generally more excited and
anxious for the contest. There is little danger that they will
be caught overlooking an opponent or taking him lightly.

2. *Team supported by him when it works hard*   Unlike the
hard-nose coach, the intense coach is prone to lavish praise
on a player when he works hard or when he succeeds. It is
not unusual, after a big win, to see him hug a player for an
outstanding effort. He genuinely appreciates a person who
is willing to match his own devotion and involvement.
Players, quite often, give the game all they have without
embarrassment. Hard work and intensity are found in this
kind of team.

3. *Coach harder worker than the athlete—proving his commitment*   It is an advantage to have the players committed
to a cause. A real sense of dedication is a very important
ingredient in the formula for success. Since there is never
any question on the part of the athlete as to the coach's
dedication, it is easier for the athlete to adopt the same
commitment.

Disadvantages

May frighten some athletes by being too demanding   The
athlete who is incapable, for whatever reason, of the same
degree of commitment as the coach may find the whole regimen too demanding or the whole scene too unreal. This will

eventually lead to some conflict and perhaps a denial of the coach's authority.

2. *Possibility of team burning out before end of season, or before crucial games* This tempo is hard to maintain. Pitched at such a high key all the time, there is always the danger that a team may burn out early. Some players feel they are being asked to produce more than they are capable of producing. They simply get too tired physically or too drained emotionally.

3. *May dislike athlete who appears lazy* A real problem can develop when the coach believes a player is incapable of or unwilling to work up to his own level of intensity. Actually the person may not be lazy, but only guilty of falling short of the coach's standard. The player may react to the situation in a negative way, however, and become more lazy as a means of defiance.

4. *Depression-prone players not handled well* The driven coach cannot understand that players might withdraw rather than become more active when faced with failure. As a result, he may think that they are lazy, or he may assume that they are quitters. They may, in fact, be only temporarily depressed.

5. *Demands may be unrealistic* This man takes competitive athletics very seriously. He is willing to do things of an extraordinarily demanding nature and spend all his time working to perfect the game, unlike some of his players who do not take the game as seriously. For them, the experience is inhibiting and continued membership on the team is undesirable.

6. *Often team members ashamed of his emotional displays* As was stated earlier, this man, due to his high degree of involvement, is likely to shout at officials, yell at his players during a game, get unusually excited, stomp his feet, and run up and down the sidelines. This may be an embarrassing

form of behavior for the players, and they may seek, in some way, to disassociate themselves from the man and the team itself.

THE "EASY-GOING" COACH

The "easy-going" coach is exactly the opposite of the driven coach. This coach appears to be suffering from no pressures whatsover. To him the whole affair is just a game—an interesting game and one he enjoys winning—but nevertheless a game.

Characteristics

1. *Does not seem to take things seriously* In this coach there is very little of the spirit which moves the hard-nose coach to be a relentless disciplinarian and very little of the quality of frenzied overemphasis which controls the intense coach. The easy-going coach is just what the term implies—relaxed, passively involved, and slightly detached.

2. *Dislikes schedules* Schedules, to this man, are seen as traps. They require a great deal of time to prepare—time that he feels may not be well spent. He prefers to leave things more open and to be able to act as his mood dictates.

3. *Does not get rattled easily* To watch this coach in action is to become convinced that he has icewater in his veins. He almost never gets upset and, at the times when other people are obviously panicked, he is completely composed and even enjoying the pressure. This is true also of his attitude toward problems which occur in practice. They are handled calmly and without emotion.

4. *Gives impression that everything is under control—at times appears lazy* Players and fans alike get the impression that matters are always well in hand. He seems to have accounted for every eventuality and is confident of the out-

come. This may be carried to an extreme and, as a result of his calm demeanor, many people are likely to get the idea that the man is actually lazy and careless about his professional duties.

Advantages

1. *Little pressure within the team*   The threat to the athlete is virtually nonexistent on this team, much the same as with the nice-guy, but to an even greater degree. The main difference between the nice-guy and the easy-going coach is the way people regard them. People are involved with the nice-guy. They make comments about his affability and charm. He is very sociable. The easy-going coach is not anti-social but perhaps asocial. To some he may even appear to be a cold person.

2. *Little griping by team about hard work*   In such a relaxed atmosphere and with the freedom from stress, it is very unlikely that the players would feel overworked.

3. *Things more easily picked up by team and questioned more*   In the relaxed atmosphere, the players seem to profit more from instruction and retain it longer than they would in an atmosphere where instruction is driven home with force and repressive measures. They regularly seek advice from the coach regarding effective methods for improving their play and are constantly receptive to his suggestions.

4. *Greater feeling of independence from coach*   The easy-going coach often has his players determine their own particular schedules. They may set their own training regulations and may set their own times. In team sports they often make team choices and, in some instances, determine strategy of play. The coach believes that the athletes will produce better if motivation grows out of their own enthusiasm. The end result is that the coach is more of a guide and consultant, and the athletes feel the game is their responsibility. As a result they feel more independent.

Disadvantages

1. *Often coach seen as inadequate* <u>Athletes are very apt to place the blame on the coach when failure is present.</u> Since he rarely appears to work hard at his job, it makes sense to most people that a low level of success is all that can be expected and all that he deserves.

2. *Coach often seen as a playboy—not interested in sports* The coach's critics theorize that anyone who is so casual about his duties, so calm under stress, and so unconcerned with real success cannot be very interested in sports and does not deserve the title and distinction of coach.

3. *Often team not in top physical condition due to lack of hard work* A team cannot be expected to be in top physical condition if it does not work hard. Under the easy-going coach, this situation is most likely to occur.

4. *Pressure not handled well by team—panic may occur* The type of pressure found in actual competition must be present in the daily practice sessions for it to be met effectively in a game. <u>In general, there is pressure-free practice.</u> The likelihood of panic under stress, then, is a strong probability under the easy-going coach.

5. *Coach often seen as uncaring* There is nothing more disheartening to athletes than the belief that the coach does not support them ardently and that the man with whom they work every day does not have the same degree of enthusiasm for the activity as they do. The athletes most certainly will lose some respect for the coach if this happens.

THE "BUSINESS-LIKE" COACH

The "business-like" coach is appearing with ever-increasing regularity on the sports scene. Coaches, in general, have always been very eager to learn. They are seldom selfish and rarely claim to have all the answers. The business-like coach, however, far surpasses the other types in techniques and ability to acquire new information. Coaching is becoming a more exact science all the time. The coach who uses all available means for accumulating information about his opponents and his own team must be considered to have an advantage if he has the ability to use the information.

Characteristics

1. *Approaches the sport in a calculating manner—very well organized* This coach approaches his job with the highest regard for organization. He leaves nothing to chance and sees to it that all assistant coaches are reliable and efficient. Detailed timetables are worked out; all available materials are used with precise care; objectives are kept in mind and are discussed often. The team's progress is continually evaluated to discover ineffective measures or weaknesses which detract from the team's success.

2. *Very logical in his approach* With the business-like coach, even small details are carefully examined before they are put into effect. He detests the thought of wasting time or taking part in any activity which does not make sense or which does not increase the team's proficiency. Players are selected on the basis of statistical proof of their ability. He amazes people with his complete knowledge of each player. He knows where the player has succeeded and where he has failed; he knows the probability of success for each play in every situation; he knows how to use this information to get the most effective performance out of his team.

3. *A cool person interpersonally* His relations with the players are most likely to be business-like. With this coach the most important thing is results. Players find that it is not easy to become close to him because the job gets in the way. The athlete who is most efficient in the execution of his

duties is the one most likely to receive the greatest recognition and acceptance. Personality has nothing to do with one's place on the team.

4 *Sharp intellectually* He is orderly, precise, and concerned with strategic advantages and usually quite sharp intellectually. He will probably score high on I.Q. tests, be a *thorough* student of the game, and be a master of all the fields of endeavor associated with athletic competition. He is an impressive speaker at alumni gatherings, popular with the press, confident of his ideals, and a "fine, clean-cut, all-American" example to the kids.

5. *Major emphasis on out-thinking the opponent* Success is knowledge of the opponent—what he is thinking, how he will react in all situations, where he places his emphasis, what success he has had in each area of play, and a familiarity with all the possible moves that he may use in his counter-attack.

Pragmatic and persevering The business-like coach is open to new ideas and methods. He wants to use what works. He is not prone to search about and indiscriminately select just any method of attack. He will also not continue in a system that has been proven ineffective. Once he is convinced that a system is sound, he will show great patience with it. He may spend years installing it slowly and methodically with the conviction that it will pay off when it is thoroughly learned.

Advantages

1. *Usually team up-to-date on new techniques* Little that is new will escape the person who takes the game as seriously as the business-like coach. In his orderly procedure, time is allotted for examination of new ideas and trends. He is always up-to-date on what is happening on all levels and in all varieties of sports.

2. *Sound and organized strategy for success*   No eventuality is overlooked and nothing is taken for granted. A significant improvement in team success is bound to occur when it is "super-prepared."

3. *Athletes' doubts dispelled and confidence developed through intelligent organization*   When athletes become convinced that the methods of preparation being used are the best and the strategy being employed is sound, team confidence must increase.

Disadvantages

1. *Feeling of unimportance by players—like pawns*   The players learn that proper execution is what is really important. They know, too, that the coaching staff is primarily concerned with this factor, often at the expense of the personal feelings of the individual player. With this knowledge, they lose some of their individuality and identity.

2. *Little concern for others on team—team spirit lacking*   Players do not often get "high" for a contest. Precision and accuracy may be intefered with, and therefore anything detracting from this will be discouraged. As it has been pointed out already, many players find that they produce at a higher level when they play with and for someone who invests *all* of himself in the activity.

3. *Hard on disorganized athletes*   An athlete who does not share the conviction that organization and careful attention to details is the key to success will find that he is not accepted by the coach. A careless or carefree athlete may be uncomfortable in this atmosphere and eventually may drop out if the diversity becomes too pronounced.

4. *Misses athletes motivated emotionally*   Obviously the emphasis is placed on the intelligent rather than the emotional approach to the realization of goals. In a highly emotional atmosphere, some players are easily and effectively moti-

vated. They may be lost in one where emotion is not present. For them, the level of success may be seriously impaired. A team having a business-like coach is not apt to have that killer instinct often necessary in a championship team. Because they function so often on an intellectual plane, they are apt to want to out-smart their opponent and, as a result, may be out-muscled or even intimidated. The coach often has a tough job trying to have them incorporate brains and muscle.

Each of the five personality types is able to more effectively handle a certain type of problem athlete. The authoritarian coach best handles the con man because he provides the necessary direction. The nice-guy coach best handles the sensitive athlete, because he is more able to provide the needed support. The unmotivated athlete who needs a push is best handled by the intense coach, while a bright and perceptive athlete works best with the easy-going coach. Finally, the business-like coach is most effective with the talented athlete who needs developing, because he is best able to provide him with the organized direction. Although each coach is *most* effective with a certain type of athlete, all coaches can be effective with each player through insight and effort.

In conclusion, we feel that the coach should remain sensitive to individual differences in his athletes. He should never lose sight of the fact that the team personality is very likely to be a reflection of his own personality. This awareness can give him an increased insight into the complex art of handling athletes and can make him more effective and sucessful in his professional life.

chapter **3**

THE ATHLETE AND HIS PERSONALITY

The coach must know the different personality types of the athletes with whom he will be working during a season, so he may effectively use the varied approaches available to him. Means and forms of communication, motivational techniques, and teaching procedures will vary in accordance with the degree to which the individual athletes and the team manifest different personality traits.

Although each athlete is uniquely motivated to compete, the athletes who are successful compose a very select group of people. The basic thing that these individuals share is talent or the ability to perform a particular skill well. A large number tend to share certain traits that typify athletic success. These traits, combined with physical talent, make possible the selection of those athletes most likely to succeed in high level competition. Athletes need not have won all their games or need not be champions to be considered successful. We define successful athletes as those who produce up to their potential. An athlete with limited talent who exhibits "winning traits" by producing up to his maximum potential is, in our minds, a successful athlete. It must be kept in mind that different sports have different requirements which, in turn, make special demands on the athlete.

This makes it difficult to talk about "athlete" in a singular way. There are, however, traits that each athlete possesses to varying degrees. The different traits and the degree to which each athlete possesses that trait determine his uniquenes. Since no two athletes are completely alike, we can only talk about the relative similarity of athletes.

Determining personality characteristics, which may have some relationship to athletic performance, is a relatively new approach in physical education. A great amount of work has been done in this area at the Institute for the Study of Athletic Motivation (ISAM) at San Jose State College under the co-directorship of Thomas A. Tutko, Bruce C. Ogilvie, and Leland Lyon.

On the basis of a large number of observations and evaluations of individual athletes, a number of personality traits related to high athletic achievement have been determined. These traits are: drive, determination, intelligence, aggression, leadership, organization, coachability, emotionality, self-confidence, mental toughness, responsibility, trust, and conscience development. Profile sheets indicating the degree to which an athlete possesses these traits have been developed. The personality traits are divided into two general areas: *desire factors* and *emotional factors*. Desire factors relate to the individual's expectations from athletics and his willingness to work toward accomplishing his goals. The emotional factors deal with the athlete's very personal attitudes and feelings about himself, his coach, and the manner in which he is being handled. Because they relate very closely to the player's personal feelings, they are greatly affected by the coach's handling techniques.

PERSONALITY CHARACTERISTICS RELATED
TO ATHLETIC MOTIVATION

Desire Factors

Drive   This is the desire to win or to be successful. The player who possesses this trait to a high degree likes to be challenged. He is very competitive, and he places winning above other things. Most likely athletics comes first in his life, and he is willing to do unpleasant things if he thinks it will help him win.

If the coach finds the athlete to be low on drive, his major objective is to help that athlete set progressively higher goals for himself. The coach must then be particularly careful to reward the athlete when he does well in his efforts to achieve these goals.

Determination The person with determination does not give up easily. He is willing to practice long and hard to achieve his goals. He is probably the first person out to practice and one of the last to leave. He spends much time working on his skills by himself, sometimes to the point of exhaustion.

If the athlete is low on determination, the coach should help him work out a schedule, which states how long he must work, what he should expect to accomplish, and how many repetitions would be required to complete the routine. The athlete must be helped to become more productive in his practice sessions.

Intelligence This factor pertains to the athlete's ability to grasp things quickly. He is able to pick up information with few repetitions, and he is free from having to labor over complex material.

Aggression The person in whom this trait is evident to a high degree thinks it is necessary to be aggressive to win. He likes to argue and is quick to criticize when someone makes a mistake. He is very concerned about not getting pushed around. He loves physical contact and is very anxious to get back at people who beat him. He rarely refrains from speaking out when he is angry.

It is very hard for some athletes to learn to be aggressive. One thing the coach can do is support and sanction any kind of aggression he observes in that athlete. He might find out from the athlete why it is hard for him to act aggressively. He must make it clear to the individual that aggression is a vital part of athletic success. The coach may even have to show the player, step-by-step, exactly how he would expect him to be aggressive in certain situations.

5 *Leadership* The athlete who possesses this characteristic likes to influence his teammates to do things his way. He enjoys the opportunity to lead his teammates and is usually good at getting what he wants from them. He likes to make decisions, is quite outspoken, and often is placed in charge of things. Also, he probably wins most of the arguments in which he participates.

The coach may help to develop leadership qualities by giving the athlete responsibilities for tasks necessary for team success. A good team is made up of a number of leaders, each with his own area of independent leadership.

6 *Organization* This characteristic enables a person to effectively place things in perspective. He is able to plan, and he is comfortable when the program is structured.

Developing the ability to organize is a matter of detailing for the athlete exactly what is expected of him. The athlete eventually will learn what to expect and, in the process, realize the importance of individual responsibility.

II **Emotional Factors**

1 *Coachability* The athlete who is coachable respects the coach and accepts his advice. This person respects training rules, accepts the leadership of the team captain, and values the coaching he receives, considering it an important part of becoming a good athlete. He feels free to talk to the coach about his ideas concerning a game. He is very likely to be a good team player.

The coach can never force anyone to respect him. He can only present to the athlete what he is and hope that the athlete respects his ideas. By being fundamentally sound, well-organized, and fair, the coach will gain the respect of most athletes. Often an athlete who seems to be uncoachable only wants to ask questions. If the coach will allow the athlete to ask questions and then answer them, he will be far more effective with the athlete than if he were to turn him off with the simple admonition to "Do what you're told." In some instances, athletes become more coachable if they know that the coach is human. A personal talk, time spent with the individual, and support for the player may be all that is necessary to bring a solution to the problems of coachability.

2. *Emotionality* This person can control his emotions and is mature and stable. He is not likely to be adversely affected by his feelings. Quite often these feelings do not even show. He is not easily depressed or frustrated by bad breaks, bad calls by the official, or by his own mistakes. A great deal of self-discipline is evident in this person's behavior. He rarely loses his temper and almost never feels picked on by other people.

Sometimes, the coach must very clearly point out to the athlete what he expects of him in terms of emotional control. For example, if the athlete appears to be under any kind of strain or pressure, and, as a result, is beginning to lose control of his feelings, the coach may attempt to find out what is causing the anxiety and remove the cause if possible. The coach may even be required to be the athlete's total emotional control.

3. *Self-confidence* This athlete is very sure of himself and his ability. He is not prone to worry about his play, to show indecisiveness, or to be upset by unexpected situations. He not only accepts criticism well from the coach, but also is very likely to speak up for what he believes both to the coach and to other players.

The coach can help the athlete build confidence by complimenting him and rewarding him for things he has done well rather than punishing him for things he has done poorly. Several short-range, obtainable goals can be set to help make the athlete feel a sense of accomplishment. After each goal has been attained, the coach and the athlete can set further goals. This process will lead to an increased self-confidence on the part of the athlete.

4. *Mental toughness* The athlete who is mentally tough is somewhat insensitive to the feelings and problems of others. He rarely gets upset when losing, playing badly, or being spoken to harshly. He is able to accept strong criticism without being hurt, and he does not require too much encouragement from the coach to be effective. This person does not depend on the team for a sense of belonging.

To develop mental toughness in a sensitive athlete, he must be informed ahead of time that he will often be required to take a tough chewing out, not with the purpose of degrading him personally, but to get across a message with strong emphasis. The goal is to make everyone more effective—not to humiliate anyone.

5. *Responsibility* This characteristic enables an athlete to accept responsibility for his actions and to work to improve his mistakes. The athlete with an overpowering sense of responsibility tends to dwell on his mistakes and to punish himself for those mistakes. He is even willing to take the blame when it is not his fault. He is willing to withstand much physical and mental pain. He will play hard even when he is injured.

When an individual does not accept any responsibility at all or is very low in guilt-proneness, the coach must very objectively show the athlete by means of films, statistics, or charts exactly what is expected of him and where he is failing. If the athlete is too high in guilt-proneness, the reverse is true. The coach must take some of the responsibility off the player's shoulders by accepting some of it himself.

6. *Trust* The athlete who possesses this characteristic to a high degree accepts people at face-value. He does not look for ulterior motives behind what others do or say; he believes what the coach says to him. Sometimes he is easily fooled by his teammates' pretenses, but most of the time he gets along extremely well with his fellow players and enjoys the competitive situation.

The coach can build trust by giving small responsibilities to the individual, by asking certain things of him, and by complimenting him when he succeeds in doing these things. The coach needs to build up trust slowly but surely. He must be careful never to undermine the player or make fun of him, because that will tear down any confidence that has been built up.

7 *Conscience development* This athlete likes to do things as correctly as possible. He will not try to bend the training rules to fit his own needs, and he places the good of the team above his own personal well-being. He is rarely late for practice, will not miss a practice session except for legitimate reasons previously discussed with the coach, and can be trusted to take very good care of the equipment and material issued to him.

Firm limits must be set for players who do not have a highly developed conscience. The coach must make it clear that if the rules are not followed, the player will have penalties imposed upon him.

ASSESSING PERSONALITY TRAITS

There are several methods of assessing the degree to which an individual athlete possesses these personality traits. The coach, himself, may subjectively rate the individual in each of the areas we have described, or he may even ask the player to rate himself. On a scale of 1 to 9, a number is circled to indicate the person's level (1 to 3 is low; 4 to 6 is average; and 7 to 9 represents a high level). In using this approach, there is, of course, a danger that the coach or the athlete may be biased.

It might be better to have an independent party evaluate the athlete, but this would involve a large amount of time in observation and evaluation, and it would also require a person who is conversant with the personality traits and with competitive athletics.

A third method, requiring a minimum amount of time, provides the coach with an objective evaluation of the athlete's personality. A test assessing these traits has been developed by Thomas Tutko, Bruce Ogilvie, and Leland Lyon of the Institute for the Study of Athletic Motivation at San Jose State College.[1] The test is called the *Athletic Motivation Inventory* (AMI). It is a paper and pencil test designed specifically to measure those traits which are related to high athletic achievement. The AMI can aid the coach in handling his athletes because it determines in which personality areas the athlete must be motivated. More specifically, the AMI gives measurements on the desire and emotional factors, as well as on the twelve individual personality dimensions. They include:

Desire factors	*Emotional factors*
Drive	Coachability
Determination	Emotionality
Aggression	Self-confidence
Leadership	Mental toughness
Organization	Responsibility
	Trust
	Conscience development

Each athlete who takes the test is compared to other athletes who participate in the same sport at the same level, i.e., high school, college, or professional. The results are reported to the coach on a nine-point scale, with a rating of one being very low in that trait, a rating of five being average, and a rating of nine being very high in that particular trait. At the bottom of the profile sheet, there is a brief description of the athlete, with emphasis on those traits which may present handling problems to the coach (see Figure 1).

In using such material as the *Athletic Motivation Inventory*, it is extremely vital that the coach apply his knowledge of each athlete in a constructive manner. If such

---

1. *Athletic Motivation Inventory*, Institute for the Study of Athletic Motivation, Thomas Tutko, Bruce Ogilvie, and Leland Lyon, Psychology Department, San Jose State College, San Jose, California.

FIGURE 1. Player Profile Sheet

NAME <u>Tom Smith</u>   TEAM <u>Basketball</u>   POSITION <u>Center</u>

1 = very low   3 = low   5 = average   7 = high   9 = very high

1. *Drive* 1 2 3 4 5 6 ⑦ 8 9
Desire to be a winner

2. *Self-confidence* 1 2 3 4 ⑤ 6 7 8 9
Sure of himself and of his ability

3. *Aggressiveness* 1 2 3 4 5 ⑥ 7 8 9
A hard hitter—willing to assert himself

4. *Coachability* 1 2 3 4 5 6 7 ⑧ 9
Willing to accept coaching

5. *Determination* 1 2 ③ 4 5 6 7 8 9
Determined—sticks with it

6. *Emotionality* 1 2 3 4 5 6 ⑦ 8 9
Can handle his feelings well

7. *Conscience development* 1 2 3 4 5 ⑥ 7 8 9
Does things as correctly as possible

8. *Trust* 1 2 ③ 4 5 6 7 8 9
Accepts people at face value

9. *Responsibility* 1 2 3 4 5 6 7 8 ⑨
Accepts responsibility—accepts blame

10. *Leadership* 1 2 3 4 5 6 7 ⑧ 9
Wants to take charge of others

11. *Mental toughness* 1 2 ③ 4 5 6 7 8 9
Can take a tough chewing out

Smith looks very good in general. There are a few areas of possible concern to the coach and athlete. He says it is quite difficult for him to stick to things over the long haul; drills requiring him to stick to things until he accomplishes a specific goal might help. He is also somewhat tender-minded and sensitive to criticism; handle him gently and try to point out his mistakes objectively and privately. He also says he does not trust others readily. Trust is an important foundation on which coaching must rest. You must be sure that everything you say to him is valid and reliable, otherwise he will only be reinforced in his mistrust. Smith might get down on himself when he makes a serious mistake, although the overall strength of his personality will probably prevent this from occurring often. If it does happen, however, you should try to take the burden of guilt off his shoulders. Smith is ambitious, reasonably sure of himself, conscientious, coachable, and mature in handling his feelings. Should motivation become a problem, he should respond well to being challenged. He would like to lead his teammates; he is a potential team leader.

information is used to degrade the athlete or becomes a basis for prejudice, it is not only destructive, but also unethical. The decision as to the ultimate use of such confidential material must be made with care. If the coach finds himself in a position of having such information, but is in doubt as to its usage, it is recommended that he seek professional assistance, in order to attain maximum effectiveness. The major aim of such material is to help the coach help the athlete to help himself.

HOW TO HANDLE PROBLEM ATHLETES

Most coaches probably have had a number of athletes who have been particularly perplexing to them—athletes with whom the coach has been unable to affect any significant change. Some athletes might be considered just odd, others as having borderline disturbances, and still others as having deep emotional problems. Athletes who have personal problems are particularly difficult for coaches to understand, because most coaches have not had the opportunity to study individual differences, especially when it comes to what might be called disturbed behavior.

There is no other area in which problem behavior is more likely to occur than in athletics. This is true for several reasons: the act of competition may have an inherent physical risk; the athlete is constantly being evaluated (as a result there is a tendency to be anxious) ; and competition produces constant stress on the participants—the more intense the competition, the greater the pressure.

A book titled *Problem Athletes and How to Handle Them*[2] by Dr. Bruce Ogilvie and Dr. Thomas A. Tutko deals specifically with the most common types of problems confronting athletes. Table 1 is a very brief description of some of the problems athletes may have, how the athlete may have become the way he is, and how the coach may be able to help the athlete.

---

2. B. C. Ogilvie and T. A. Tutko, *Problem Athletes and How To Handle Them* (London, England: Pelham Books, 1966).

TABLE 1. Handling Problem Athletes

Description	Etiology	Handling
Athlete who resists coaching This athlete often has a better answer than the coach for doing things; he will not listen, or does just the opposite of what the coach asks him to do. Sometimes the athlete openly rebels. He refuses to do anything at all.	The athlete may have had distasteful encounters with authority figures (usually the father figure), and now he is rebelling against any authority. The rebellion may be of a very subtle type. That is, he may say "yes," promise to do what he is asked to do, and then do the opposite. The authority figure has either forced or coerced the person into doing something he never felt a part of, or responsible for. As a result, the athlete does not trust or believe in the coach. The father figure may not have been present, and the athlete now is acting out his resentment.	The most common form of handling is to talk with the individual, get to know him, and build a trust. Reassuring him may not be easy, but it must be done to achieve success. Sometimes the athlete simply wants to ask questions and to find out what the limits are, and if the coach will stand behind what he says. In more severe cases it may be a direct challenge, and a confrontation is necessary. If the athlete gets too resistive, the coach may have to resort to ignoring him. He should handle him by behavioral means rather than verbally. He should direct the athlete by gestures or expressions and avoid speaking to him or answering his questions. When the athlete sees this kind of treatment he may become quite disturbed by it and realize that his method of resistance is not effective.

TABLE 1. (Continued)

Description	Etiology	Handling
Con Man He is very selfish, tries to get his way, and is narcissistic. He does not want to cooperate unless he gets his share of glory. He is often very ingratiating. He talks nicely, and before long, everybody is doing something for him. Later, he violates rules and regulations and has excuses for doing so. He seems to have his own rules. He is not necessarily rebellious, but at times works people against each other to get what he wants.	This person has not had limits set on his behavior. He has been overly mothered or babied. What he did was always right—he could never do wrong. As a result, he has grown up in an unrealistic world. There are no confines for him—the rules do not apply to him.	The coach must make it clear that there are definable limits and punishments for breaking the rules. There are sensitive con men and tough-minded con men. The sensitive con man needs to be told what the limits and punishments are in a very fatherly, straightforward way; the tough-minded con man needs to be told in a rather harsh way.
Hyper-anxious or psyched-out athlete This is the athlete who is described as "flaky." He is unpredictable—great one day, poor the next. He falls apart at times when he is being depended on most. No one is ever quite sure what is going to happen with this athlete. He gets too anxious before a game.	These individuals come from backgrounds where life was unpredictable. Things were good one time, bad the next. They found early in life whatever they tried was effective one time, ineffective another. As a result, they feel they live in an unpredictable world. They are not quite sure what to expect. They go totally on their whims and feeling at the moment.	The coach needs to make his expectations very clear so the athlete will know that he is supported if he wins or loses. He needs to know that he is expected to put out his very best. Anxiety is the chief problem. If he can help the athlete through anxious moments with support, he may change his pattern of unpredictability. Just talking to him may do it. Sometimes, changing the player's assignment is necessary.

52

Description	Etiology	Handling
Success-phobic athlete This is the athlete whose biggest problem is not the fear of failing, but the fear of succeeding. It is as though he is not grown up enough to deal with the responsibility which comes from success.	In the past, this person has found that success has only brought a form of rejection or a loss of success to others. If he did well, others became jealous. As a result, winning does not lead to joy, but rather to pain.	The athlete must be made to feel that he is solely responsible for his own actions. If he does well in practice, the coach should see to it that he receives the proper amount of credit. By the same token, the athlete should accept the responsibility for his failure. The biggest fear with this athlete is that when he gets on top, he may tend to follow the good performance with a poor one. He will probably experience a letdown during the contest at some time. At the time he does well, he needs the coach's support and backing.
Injury-prone athlete There are several different types. One type plays the game with reckless abandon and actually gets injured often.	These are the people who, in the past, have been made heroes for being savage-like or daredevilish when they play. Perhaps their only claim to fame came through injuries.	The coach must be the protecting source for the athlete and no longer reward his self-sacrificing behavior.

TABLE 1. (Continued)

Description	Etiology	Handling
Malingerer This is the person who lies about an injury and knows he is lying. He is a "game" athlete and not a "practice" athlete. He will feign an injury to get out of practice.	These people are quite immature and childlike. They use infantile ways of getting out of responsibility or situations which might lead to pain. Sometimes they are con men because they have been protected from facing reality.	If the coach suspects the athlete of malingering, he should see to it that the athlete does not get the rewards enjoyed by the other members of the team.
Psychosomatic injury With this type of athlete, the psychological pain brings about physical pain. There is actually nothing physically wrong with the athlete, but he will develop the symptoms of an ulcer, or a migraine headache, back pain, or other recurring pseudo injuries. These symptoms are caused by the athlete's anxiety about the contest. The real fear is not of injury itself, but it is a fear of the anxiety that accompanies certain situations. This anxiety may result from a fear of not doing well, losing, or being punished. Through psychologically feigning injury, the athlete can escape the mental pain associated with the contest.	These people have been overly protected as children. They have been kept out of potentially dangerous situations by parental figures.	The coach must attack the anxiety. He can support them and help them to not feel so bad over losses or failure. All he should expect from them is that they do their very best. If they know this, it will help to ease their anxiety.

Description	Etiology	Handling
Withdrawn or suspicious athlete This is the athlete who stays by himself. He does not like to get mixed up with the other members of the team in any of their activities.	This person has probably been hurt by close interpersonal relationships. He has either been let down, insulted, or not supported by others. When he became close to others, they hurt him in some way. As a result, he does not trust other people.	The coach should be very straightforward and factual with this athlete. Never lie to him, build him up falsely, or say anything to him that is not true. Support him. Encourage him to interact with others, but do not force him to do so. It is important that the coach shows that he trusts this person. The suspicious athlete will take quite some time to overcome his problem.
Depression-prone athlete This athlete takes a loss much more severely than others. He may be depressed for several days. He gets off by himself to sulk and is unable to pull out of the state of depression.	In the past, no one has shown faith in him. He has been made fun of or laughed at. His inadequacies were continually pointed out to him. When the athlete is depressed he has turned the anger inward and is punishing himself.	The coach must take some of the responsibility off of this athlete's shoulders. He can point out to the player that it is just as much the coach's fault as the player's. He can support him by saying things like, "Look, it's O.K. We all have bad days. Things like that happen to everyone. Don't let it bother you."

In the handling of any athlete, individual treatment makes the big difference between long range success and failure. The coach should be concerned for the athlete as a *person*. By complimenting the athlete when he does well, the coach will be better able to establish good habits and create in the players the proper feelings about themselves and the team. The problems described in Table 1 may be of a relatively minor intensity, or they may be quite severe. If the coach finds himself confronted with a situation in which the problem has become so severe that it is interfering with many aspects of the athlete's life, it is strongly recommended that the coach seek professional advice about handling the athlete, or he should have the athlete get professional help. In most schools and colleges, counseling services are available, and the coach should use them whenever possible.

The coach must never forget what his attitudes are toward the different aspects of an athlete's personality, because they will determine the manner and degree of success he will have with each individual. Of course, the handling of any athlete goes well beyond the mouthing of words. It involves, more specifically, the *behavior* of the coach, which shows a perception of, an interest in, and a genuine concern for the athlete.

chapter **4**

LEVELS OF COACHING

The four levels of athletic participation to be dealt with in this chapter are preadolescent, adolescent, college, and professional. Just as the development of athletic skills varies at each of these levels (more fundamental with the younger child—more technical and sophisticated with the older athlete), there are different emotional and psychological needs to be met at each level. At any level, the coach can be true to his own personality, but he also should be in tune with the needs of the individuals with whom he will be working to gain the best results for all concerned. Although there are individual differences within each of the various levels, there are common problems faced by athletes at each level.

PREADOLESCENT

Preadolescence is the period in which the personality of the child is really beginning to form. He is developing attitudes about many things—authority, adults, athletics, competition, responsibility, and rules. A boy's personality may be in a constant state of flux, because he is trying to establish a sense of identity. At this level of development and for the first time in his life, he may come into contact with others in a competitive environment. If his first athletic experience makes him feel worthwhile, and if this feeling is carried over into other areas, the experience will have been positive.

At this stage, it is vital for the coach to be more concerned with the growth of the individual than with winning games. Learning to handle losing is far more important for children than learning to handle winning. In working with the child at this age, the coach must see as his major goal the development of the *person*. He has a duty to help the individual form a positive attitude toward physical exercise and play. At this time, it is the process of learning the fundamentals of participation—not winning games—that is the essential end-product of athletic competition.

In the preadolescent stage, the game should really be played for fun. Unfortunately, this is not always possible. Some Little League "adults," for example, do not allow children to play for the enjoyment of the sport. The overzealous parents place undue stress on the youngsters and consequently destroy the atmosphere of friendly competition.

The anxiety faced by the individual at this level is likely to be more pronounced than at any other time in his athletic career. If, for example, he is not particularly talented or interested in the sport and is being pushed by an ambitious parent, he may suffer greatly—not knowing whether to continue and try to please his parents or to quit and please himself. An understanding coach can make this situation much more bearable. On the other hand, if the coach is similarly ambitious for the child, the activity may become intolerable for him. He will probably give up athletics at the first opportunity.

Just from the point of view of attitude toward athletics, the handling at this time is critical. Will the athletic experience be positive or negative? Will the individual continue to participate? A fundamental goal of every coach, therefore, should be to make athletic participation a rewarding experience. Even if the boy goes no further in his athletic career, the coach has an obligation to make the involvement a valuable part of the growing-up process. The coach commits a grave injustice when he develops the "star" at the expense of the rest of the team, or when he concentrates only on winning games.

Preadolescence is the period in which children have their first critical experiences outside the school. During this time, they are being taught something by which many people will assess them. It is probable that the coach is the first male authority figure of importance outside the home, and it may be the first time the child has been placed on exhibit for outsiders to evaluate.

Although the need to build confidence may be apparent in all stages, it is most important for the preadolescent. He does not have a backlog of information about how the sport is to be played, nor previous experience upon which to base his conduct in the sport, as do high school, college, and professional athletes. The coach must give encouragement to the preadolescent, until he is able to build up his own confidence through actual participation in and knowledge of the sport.

The coach must keep in mind the fact that the complexities of the game are totally incomprehensible to a beginner. At this age the child is quite prone to make mistakes and lose his poise, because he has had little experience. There is nothing for him to build on if the opportunity has not been presented to him before. The situation is comparable to teaching a child to use algebra before he has had simple arithmetic. The coach should be careful to protect him from being too severely "wounded" by embarrassment and to prevent him from being placed in a situation that will cause stress he cannot handle. If stress does occur, the coach should make every effort to support the boy after he has failed.

The preadolescent is apt to be frightened if the sport places him in some physical danger. If he has been hit by a baseball, it may be nearly impossible for him to stand at the plate and face a fast pitcher. For example, a father, with good intentions, forced his son to stand at the plate while he threw balls close to him in an effort to help the boy overcome his fear. This, of course, only intensified the fear and soon led to the boy's complete withdrawal from baseball.

The preadolescent has less effective ways of dealing with the anxiety created by the stresses resulting from athletics. He may not have learned how to rationalize a poor performance, to find solace in a successful aspect of his play, or to find a scapegoat, as older players do. The preadolescent is more inclined to respond to the immediate success or failure than to look at the long range picture. At this point, the concept of momentum is outside his comprehension.

At this stage, the boy is more likely to be playing for a number of reasons other than enjoyment of the sport—his buddies are playing; there are nice uniforms, which serve as an important status symbol; players get their names in the paper occasionally; parents are pushing him; he idolizes a sports personality; or he fantasizes about what he can do in a heroic way.

The preadolescent is easily affected by outside influences. If the crowd is booing him, he is more apt to take it personally. As he grows older, he will come to understand and withstand these factors, but at this level, they may be too much for him to handle. He may become highly depressed, break down in tears, or try to withdraw entirely from the situation.

The coach may be confronted with outbursts of severe immaturity at this level, and he must be prepared for them. In a few cases, it might help to say things like "Be grown up," "Don't cry," or "Be a man," but saying such things is much more likely to cause serious problems in many other areas. The boy is probably trying to control his emotions and act "grown-up" already, but the importance of the failure is just too much for him to handle. He needs someone to help him and support him—someone who will understand the emotions he is experiencing and share the hurt. It is to be expected that the child will feel encouraged when the crowd cheers him, but he is also just as likely to feel very depressed when the crowd boos him. Unless he is helped through these difficult periods, he may drop out of the competitive situation entirely. In younger children, the intensity of the emotions are magnified, since the child has not had much of an opportunity to face extremely emotional situations.

Parental evaluation carries a great deal of weight with the preadolescent. If the child is being viewed by parents and fails, he will need much support. The coach should be aware of the boy who is being pushed and pressured by others and be prepared to relieve this pressure whenever possible. If, for example, the coach knows that the father of the boy is a former athlete, he might carefully check to see if there is any pressure on the child to "follow in his dad's footsteps."

The coach may even choose to record a few behavioral patterns of the boy's parents to help determine their attitudes. For example:

1. How often is the parent present at practice?
2. What is his attitude about practice?
3. Is the parent present at all games?
4. What is his behavior during a game—excited or relaxed? Is he supportive or angry with the child when he fails?
5. How many times does the parent make contact with the coach? What are his expressed concerns?
6. Does the parent feel the child never does anything wrong?
7. Does the parent feel the child never does anything right?

Dealing with parents can be a very delicate matter. It is quite probable that this is the period in which the greatest amount of conflict between the parents and the coach will arise. The coach must be prepared both to ease the anxieties of over-protective parents and to subtly manipulate the passions of ambitious parents. If he can establish a rapport with all parents—particularly with those who have some doubts about him—he has accomplished a monumental feat.

The parents' meeting is one of the best techniques available to the coach for making his ideas known and for gaining parental support. It also provides the coach with an excellent opportunity to ease parents' minds about the dangers their child faces (see Chapter 10 for a discussion of outside influences on the athlete).

With anxious parents, the coach can ease their concern by explaining his techniques and methods of protection. By providing these parents with the assurance that he places the child's welfare above all else, he can win their confidence and support. As for the situation with the ambitious parents, the focus of attention here should become the child. By talking with the boy, gaining his confidence, and explaining to him that he is under no pressure to perform beyond his capacity, the problem can be alleviated. The coach should explain to the boy that he can ask no more of a player than his best. At no time will the performance on the field affect the coach's regard for the youngster.

Unfortunately, the coaches who are not effective with the preadolescent all too often fall into one of two categories: the former athlete who is re-living his days of glory through the children—semi-knowledgeable in the sport, but very deficient in the techniques of handling children; and the "dedicated father," wonderfully enthusiastic and anxious to give kids what they need, but almost totally ignorant of the fundamentals of the sport. On the one hand, the team members are indelicately whipped into shape without much regard for their feelings. On the other hand, a healthy atmosphere for emotional growth is established, but little fundamental skill is developed. It is to be hoped that were a choice between the two types available, the latter would be given precedence, because he adheres to most of the basic principles necessary for coaching the preadolescent:

1. Be concerned with the person—not the performance.
2. Understand and attempt to meet the needs of the child.
3. Make athletic participation a positive experience.
4. Protect and support the child in situations he is not prepared to handle.
5. Focus on small but meaningful goals, reinforced by rewards.

ADOLESCENT

Adolescence is a testing period, and the athletic world sometimes becomes the testing ground. The coach, by the very nature of his personality, may become the person with whom the athlete identifies—the ideal, a parental figure, or an authority to rebel against.

At this stage, the child has a strong need for identification. The adolescent is trying to find a strong, stable figure with whom to identify. At this age, he has sports heroes. There are instances when the coach himself becomes the model, especially if the boy has come from a relatively unstable background.

While adolescents are seeking identity as members of a team, it is also a time of subtle rebellion. The players may defy the rules as cleverly as possible (coming three minutes late to the meeting, shooting 20 free-throws instead of 25, or running one less lap than was required). Individuals are caught up in a search for themselves or for their future. On the one hand, the coach may be put on a pedestal, but at the same time the player rebels against him.

One of the reasons for the confusion and frustration is that in our culture there is no clearly defined instance where we pass from adolescence to adulthood. In some cultures, there are rituals or rites which definitely mark the end of adolescence and the beginning of manhood. In our society, however, there is really no such thing. The athletic field may be seen as the testing ground for adulthood or more specifically, as a test of masculinity.

The adolescent finds it difficult to place athletics in the proper perspective. Is it play or is it work? Is it maturity or is it immaturity? Where do athletics and play fit into our general scheme of things? Some people see athletics as child's play, while others see it as very serious business. This is a major question which adolescents face. Is high school football, for example, a serious endeavor, or merely a game to be played for fun? Peer pressure reaches its peak at this point. A player is very likely to be affected by his own teammates, his school, his girlfriend, and his buddies.

Talent begins to separate individuals. For the first time, the boy may not have equal playing time in athletic participation. It is now much more apparent who is talented, and a premium is placed on that talent. This poses another problem—if the person had his heart set on succeeding in athletics, and now finds that he does not have sufficient talent, it is a crushing blow. This may cause him to feel incapable in other areas also. It may even intensify problems at home.

Many times the adolescent's future is in doubt. He is likely to change his goals several times. He is unsure of himself and he is searching for some answers to his future. Choice of college, major, future goals, athletic involvement, and military obligation are all very serious issues he must face.

The player's feelings about his athletic future may cause him to behave in a variety of ways. If he is talented, he may be anxious about his choice of colleges. If he is not, he may become despondent, knowing that this is the end of his athletic career. The knowledge that he is to be deprived of something he enjoys very much is terribly discomforting.

The "super-star" may have a great deal of hostility directed at him because he is going to get the opportunity to go on and participate in an activity which will be denied to other members of the team. Secretly, the other players feel, "I'm at the height of my career now—you're going on to receive future recognition. It's a stepping stone for you— it's my whole career!"

Handling the adolescent is the most difficult coaching problem. The major reason for this is that the coach himself will be tested. The athletes will be paying close attention to the coach as a person. The adolescents will want to know if the coach will accept them for what they are or whether he wants them to be something else to fulfill his own needs.

In order for the coach to effectively handle adolescents, certain elements of his behavior are vital. The following are a few of the essential elements:

The coach must be a model of what he says. If he professes one thing, yet practices another, he will be tagged a "fake" and his words will mean little. For example, if he forbids his athletes from swearing and yet does so himself, his double standard will force the adolescents to regard him as a less capable leader, because he cannot practice what he preaches.

The coach must be willing to listen to and consider seriously the needs of each athlete. To be left out in a period during which he is attempting to establish identity can be destructive to the adolescent. In many instances, his suggestions may simply indicate his attempt to be heard rather than a demand that his ideas be followed. If the coach listens, the athlete will feel his identity is recognized. If the coach fails to listen and ignores him, the athlete loses his identity. The coach must be prepared to hear many suggestions that are nearly impossible, and yet he must have the patience to point out the inappropriateness of the suggestions. Moreover, he must do this in an emphatic manner, letting the athlete know he has considered his opinion. The coach may get around this problem ahead of time by having an "open door" policy for the athlete or a "suggestion box." In this way, the athlete will have a degree of assurance that he will be heard.

The coach must never attempt to deceive or mislead the athlete. There are those times when the coach may be perplexed or baffled by the team situation. Rather than presenting a facade indicating that there are no problems or that things are going well, he may present the situation to the athletes asking for opinions from them. These periods of openness will reassure the athletes that they will be able to share in team decisions and that they are part of the unit. If this is done, however, it is important that the coach reassure the team that a solution will be found and that the team need not feel the situation is hopeless or insoluble. It is simply that there is a period of momentary blockage or standstill.

The coach must be prepared for and willing to accept periods during which the athletes may attempt wild, off-beat, and sometimes blatantly exhibitionistic behaviors. Whether it be dress, personal grooming, odd mannerisms, or language, it is a period of seeking identity, and these behaviors are all a part of this period. The coach is in a position to help the athlete establish a sense of identity with the team. If he is successful in doing that, the other behaviors will be minimized or dropped altogether. Failing to let the adolescents have their own identity can only lead to problems.

The coach must try to assume the role of a kind, considerate, empathic father figure rather than a lord and master. If this can be done while at the same time setting limits and enforcing the rules and regulations of the team, the coach can provide a "growing up" experience for his athletes.

COLLEGE

When the individual reaches college, he may be required to be truly independent for the first time in his life. For many, this independence is confusing and difficult to handle. In this situation, the athlete may turn to the coach for advice and counsel.

In college, the athlete becomes acutely aware of the fact that he is there because of his talent. This places him under a new kind of pressure from that experienced in high school. His presence in high school did not depend on his athletic ability; in college, it may. It is also likely that he was a campus celebrity in high school, while in college he may easily get lost and be rather obscure unless he is very special. The individual must make the personal adjustment by forming a sense of identity along with feelings of independence. The coach can help.

The younger the person, the more apt he is to fantasize about his ability and his chances to become a famous athlete. By the time he reaches college, the individual is more realistic about his abilities as an athlete, and he is less likely to suffer from any delusions. Whether he likes it or not, he must make some serious judgments about his future in athletics. It becomes obvious to everyone that either he is a potential professional athlete or he is not. Other "dreams" he held during his youth (that he would grow larger, develop speed, strength, and maturity) must fade. He may shift his focus away from becoming a participating athlete, but still stay in the same area by thinking about becoming a coach or a physical educator.

This is the stage in which the individual broadens his interests and allegiances. The athlete begins to focus on things outside the athletic experience such as a future profession, goals, and marriage.

With the more realistic appraisal of his future in athletics, along with his widening interests, the individual's enthusiasm for athletics may begin to wane. As a matter of fact, some colleges find the athlete they recruited turning to thoughts of his future at the expense of his sport.

The coach must become aware of these intense pressures on the athlete and do what he can to help relieve them. Coaches at this level are apt to neglect the personal touch and concentrate on the development of athletic talent. To the individual, the coaching staff may appear to be business-like and not interested in providing him with the personal touch he was accustomed to in high school. If the athlete is being used solely for his talent, and he becomes aware of it, he is very likely to be resentful. The resentment may manifest itself in poorer performances or in a generally negative attitude. In some instances he may become openly rebellious.

Both the coach and the player have a responsibility to each other. Whether or not the athlete is receiving an athletic scholarship, he has a responsibility to the team and to the coach; the coach has a professional responsibility to provide the individual athlete with the best set of circumstances under which he can grow and prosper. If either uses the other selfishly, there is bound to be some conflict.

The coach should feel an obligation to help the athlete obtain his degree and even to help the person get started in the direction of his choice. From the beginning of the player–coach relationship, an awareness of each other's individuality will help. The coach is in a position initially to provide comfort, reassurance, and guidance to an individual who may be insecure in the new environment.

An information sheet on the player will help the coach relate to the individual outside the competitive situation. He should attempt to discover the player's outside interests, find out his goals, and gain an insight into his personality. He can then keep the boy informed on job possibilities, help him to follow up on his interests and achieve his future goals (see Chapter 5 for a discussion on communicating with the athlete).

PROFESSIONAL

For the first time in the athlete's career, perhaps, winning becomes paramount. The status of almost everyone in the organization depends upon the won-lost record. Failure can produce feelings of agonizing depression, pure panic, or complete worthlessness.

Athletics are no longer as voluntary as they were in the past. The athlete now assumes it as a job, with regular hours and responsibilities for which he is paid a living wage. He must assume the regular duties of an adult while still performing in an area that many others still consider play.

For many, it is the first time in their lives that they are confronted with talent equal to, or greater than, their own. They must adjust to being "just another athlete" rather than an individual who stands out on the team. To some, this may be a devastating blow, and they would prefer to withdraw from participation rather than be average.

On the professional level, it immediately becomes clear to the individual that his position rests solely on his talent as an athlete. This may produce a feeling of doubt and even resentment if the person is not made to feel special in some way outside the athletic experience. He must not be made to think he is being looked upon as merchandise, to be dealt with at the whims of the owners and coaches.

There is a common belief that money is the sole source of motivation in professional athletics. It may only be a reflection of the athlete's value to the team, and the value to the team is often determined by the nature of the sport. For example, a quarterback is more valuable than an offensive lineman. Money reflects the player's importance to the team. Without it, the player would still need some indication of his relative value to the team.

Essentially, there are three ways in which a professional athlete's importance is measured: by the money he receives; whether he plays for a winning team; and by the awards he receives or by the records he sets.

A professional athlete finds himself in a somewhat unique position. In his professional life he still continues to be compared with others in his class. The large bulk of the population escapes that competitive rat-race. Others do not depend upon all-pro honors or an MVP award to maintain or create status.

More personal touches are needed in professional athletics to help give the athlete a feeling of importance and value. If the management were to send birthday messages to the wife and children, letters of support to off-season employers, and maintain contact throughout the year with the athletes on personal and professional matters, they would greatly strengthen their relationship with the individual.

In summary, while athletes play for different reasons at different times in their life, they never outgrow the need to be treated as individuals. To achieve true success as a leader of men, the coach must never lose sight of this very important fact.

chapter **5**

COMMUNICATION

In working with an athlete, a major portion of the coach's time will be spent communicating to that athlete what is expected of him. Failure to do so correctly will result in confusion and frustration on the part of both parties and may even lead to alienation and separation of coach and athlete.

In truth, without communication in all aspects of human intercourse, one faces grave problems. The coach, dealing as he does on such an intense basis with his players, faces an especially difficult task. He must not only recognize that certain players need special kinds of handling and special forms of communication, but he must also *provide* the handling and the special communication. The methods of handling individuals to fit their special psychological needs is as important as the techniques of teaching athletic skills to conform to the individual's physical abilities. In either instance, the coach's ability to communicate effectively with the athlete is a key factor in the success of his players.

FORMS OF COMMUNICATION

Information Giving

This involves not only the teaching of physical skills, but also includes such things as philosophy, strategy, game plans, and directions. Even with direct orders, the players will ask questions. Hopefully, the coach will have answers to their questions, but it is even more important that the coach be receptive to questions. If he cuts off communication, he may appear to be stubborn and lose the respect of his players. The more questions the coach allows and answers successfully early in the season, the fewer questions there will be as the players learn to trust his judgment. The more willing a coach is to justify his decisions, the more readily a team will respond. The team will realize that the coach is making realistic, not arbitrary, demands. "With nobody out and a runner on first, hit the ball to the right side *because* . . ." "Don't ever get more than five yards behind him *because* . . ." "We're going to use the Okie defense *because* . . ."

Now, what if the athlete asks a question the coach cannot answer? It is best for him to be honest and say, "I really don't know, but it's my feeling that this method is best." If he brings up something the coach had not considered, a response like, "I really hadn't considered that possibility, but I'm glad that it came up" will win the coach a great deal of personal respect. There are several ways to give information to an athlete:

Direct order The direct order *specifically* states what the coach expects of the athlete with no equivocation, such as "Run the Belly Series against the Eagle defense," or "Take a strike," or "Jones, you take Number 19 and have Tom take your man"—all involving someone being told specifically what to do, or how to do it, and dealing with an immediate situation.

Lecture The lecture has a much broader scope than the direct order, and it usually involves a *general* rather than a specific concept, for example: covering changes in the rules; giving information about last year's team; explaining the reasons for selecting a certain defense.

Demonstration The demonstration involves action—some type of physical behavior demonstrated by the coach as an example of how the player should perform. Even when the coach demonstrates, the players empathize and, so, are involved.

Analysis In analysis, the subject is broken down to its fundamental units and then built back up again to see how it succeeds or fails. Films, charts, graphs, and diagrams may be used by the coach to aid in analysis.

Information Getting

The prime purpose here is to get feedback from individual players or from the team in general about an area or subject of which the coach is in doubt. The coach should encourage his players to use the following approaches:

Suggestion This has to do with *specific* ideas. Such statements as "Coach, the draw should go, because they're starting to blow the linebackers," or "I should be able to muscle up inside now that White has four fouls," or "Maybe you should talk to Fred, Coach. He's thinking about quitting." The player should communicate feelings or ideas about specific situations important to the team that he feels the coach may not be fully informed about.

Discussion This is a broader form of communication than suggestion. It calls for some type of response on the part of two or more parties who give and receive information or clarify points of view.

Again, in dealing with the members of a team, a coach must be prepared to work with a wide variety of personality types. He will encounter the individual characteristics of aggressiveness, coachability, ambition, industriousness, toughness, and self-confidence. In general, these are "good" traits and, with players who exhibit them, any of the aforementioned forms of communication will be effective. When the athletes do not have special problems, they do not need special communication. The problem athletes, however, do need a more sensitive type of communication. The coach must compensate for their lack of "good" traits by avoiding certain forms of communication which, for the athlete, would be bad, and by using the forms which will best answer the player's needs.

Personality Conflicts

The coach's personality plays a big part in communication. When he runs across a player who is very similar to himself, he is likely to be either very successful or very unsuccessful with him. More often than not, he is likely to be unsuccessful if he has been some kind of a problem athlete himself. And when a "problem coach" gets to an athlete who suffers from the same problem as the coach, there is a very high probability that the coach will be unable to handle the player successfully or communicate with him effectively. For example, rebellious coaches usually do not get along with rebellious players. They simply cannot stand their own kind. Hyper-sensitive or hyper-anxious types only make a coach of the same type more anxious or more sensitive. It is harder for the coach to handle these problems, because he has never really been able to deal with them in himself, and he is threatened by their existence in the athlete. "Positive" types best coach their own types (aggressive coaches work well with aggressive players; confident coaches like confident athletes, etc.), but the coach who has had problems often punishes in his own players what is really a problem in himself. Table 2 is an outline of the recommended procedures for communication with the types of athletes discussed in Chapter 3.

STYLES OF COMMUNICATION

In addition to the forms of communication already described, there are several positions a coach may take with a player. The role assumed by the coach will incorporate a certain style or manner of behavior. Adjusting to the coach's style and personality will not be too much of a problem for most players, but for the problem athlete this may be a major dilemma.

"Style" may be divided into two categories. The first includes approaches that remain constant throughout the duration of a coach's relationship with the different types of problem athletes on his team, and the second includes the styles of communication that vary according to the situation and to the mood of the coach.

Constant Styles of Communication Used with Problem Athletes

Firm The coach employs a forceful manner in his directions to an athlete. The coach makes his position unequivocally clear to the player and establishes definite rules and limitations. In this situation penalties are implied by the manner of communication. This style is most effective with the con man who must have specific and consistent direction. Firmness is synonymous here with consistency. If you give the con man five rules, he subtly will break all five in time. He must be told what the penalty will be after he has broken the rule, and the coach must carefully adhere to his word. A coach, of course, can be both firm and supportive at the same time. "I know it's hard, but this is what I want you to do nevertheless."

Supportive The coach backs the athlete in whatever direction he wants to go. For example, if the athlete says, "I'm playing a lousy game, Coach," the coach, in using the supportive approach, would reply, "You seem to be having some

TABLE 2. Communicating with Problem Athletes

	Manipulator (Con Man)	Hyper-Anxious (Sensitive)	Suspicious (Withdrawn)	Rebellious (Uncoachable)	Depression-prone (In a shell)
Direct Order	Best communication form. Tell him exactly what you want. If you leave anything up to him, he has an excuse. Be *specific* and *direct* in your order.	Makes him more nervous. He responds to a direct order, but it must be stated in a fatherly or in a friendly style.	Best form of communication.	He has an excuse. He knows a better way already or he will find a better way. He is not conning; he is just battling the order.	Makes him feel he has goofed. It should be delivered in a style which indicates it is going to make him better as opposed to a style which feels points out he is incapable.
Suggestion	He is apt to manipulate the suggestion to mean what he wants and to use it for his own ends.	Best form of communication.	Does not volunteer very much. He stays to himself.	Recommended form of communication.	Recommended form of communication.
Discussion	Makes him more of a con man. Avoid.	Excellent form of communication.	The same as suggestion. When he gives, it is like giving something of himself.	Recommended form of communication.	Recommended form of communication.

76

Lecture	Much the same as suggestion. He hears only what he wants.	He responds positively. It helps him reduce anxiety.	Responds well. Nothing is expected of him because he only has to take notes.	He questions the lecture.	This is O.K. for him. It is not too much of a problem for him.
Demonstration	Use him in the demonstration because he is usually a showman and will do a good job and like it. The only one of the problem types you want to use for demonstration.	Do not use this person in demonstration. It makes him more anxious (unless it is very simple and he cannot miss having success).	He wonders why he is being picked out and this just adds to his suspiciousness.	He finds flaws in whatever is done. Use him if he has a worthwhile plan. If you ask him to demonstrate and he doesn't agree, he will do it badly to show it will not work.	He would be terrified of making a mistake. Avoid.
Analysis	Do not focus on him. He is good at coming up with an alibi or excuse. He feels he does nothing wrong. Use others to show him; even then he probably will not listen.	Do not use him. It adds to his tension.	He thinks you are picking on him again.	If he is making the mistake, then it puts him on the spot and he does not like it. Ask him what his evaluation is (discussion technique).	It is the last thing you want to do because you are pointing out to him that he's blowing it, and it causes him much pain.

trouble. What do *you* think is the problem?" If the player's answer is "I think I need more rest," the coach might say, "I didn't know you needed the rest," or "Maybe you are tired. Why don't you sit down for a while."

In effect, the coach draws out the feelings of the player and supports them. This is the recommended style of communication with the hyper-anxious athlete who constantly needs reassurance and understanding from the coach.

Fatherly   The coach is concerned with the person—he takes over for him and looks after him. This approach is used with the player who flares up, gets out of control, and causes some trouble. When this happens, the coach shows concern for him by saying "I know you're angry and this has been very hard for you, but we'll have to have some kind of control here." In the supportive style, feelings are drawn from the player; in the fatherly style, the coach provides the player with the feelings.

Friendly   The coach is a buddy to the player—he asks how things are going, jokes with him, or makes references to personal experiences shared by the two. Supportive is recognition of the person's needs, while friendly is recognition of the person. The friendly approach works well with all but the con man and the suspicious athletes. Often coaches are frightened of using a friendly approach. The coach fears it will result in a lack of respect if he places himself on the level of the athlete. The coach must feel confident in his role as the leader and must not allow the friendship to interfere with his decisions. If he does, he will lose the respect of the players and the team. He must firmly establish, very early in the relationship, that the friendship will in no way interfere with his role as leader.

Withdrawn   The coach uses this only in extreme cases. In effect, it communicates to the player that the coach does not want to communicate. An excellent example of this method is a coach's decision not to go into the locker room with the team at halftime, when he feels that they are playing a particularly poor game. It is a form of rejection, the purpose being to get the players to come to the coach, rather than the coach going to the players.

This style may be used with the rebellious athlete who is negative to the point of being destructive to the team. This person asks questions not for the answer but to destroy the authority figure whom he hates. Complete withdrawal from this type is very effective. For example, with a player who was almost totally uncoachable, every statement made by the coach was met with a question or with a belittling remark. The coach's judgment was constantly challenged, and the player almost never responded to advice and help. The withdrawal technique was used to the degree of the coach's pretending the player did not exist. Such methods as looking through him when talking to the team, never speaking to him or using his name (employing hand signals to direct him where to go if he was to enter the game, etc.), and being neither critical nor complimentary nor even aware of his play, produced amazing results in a rather short period of time. The player not only sought the acceptance of the coach, but he made many very positive contributions to the team and exhibited some excellent leadership qualities during the remainder of the season. What seemed like an impossible problem was solved in a very simple way when the correct method was used.

The coach, of course, may encounter some rebel athletes of a different nature who do not present such a serious problem. They only want attention and recognition and, when they receive it, they are satisfied.

Flexible Styles of Communication
Used with All Athletes

The term "flexible" suggests that factors are present during a season which cause a coach to change his attitude and demeanor. These changes in the coach are temporary and responsive to conditions and situations that arise, and they often depend upon the feelings of the coach at a specific moment. Some of these styles may be used in a calculating way—that is, the coach may assume a manner that is designed to evoke a certain response from the team or to create a desired feeling among the players.

Humor   There will be several times during the season when tension and stress appear—during an important game, a moment of great anxiety within a game, or a crucial demand placed on an individual—all these call for some means of reducing the emotional stress if the team is to realize its greatest potential. Humor, if handled well, can be an extremely effective means of providing this outlet.

When it is obvious to the coach that the athletes are working under great duress—"tight" or "psyched" as the players call it—a well-timed joke or humorous allusion to some unrelated incident, activity, or person, not only distracts the players' attention from the element causing the stress, but also tends to bring about a closeness between players.

If the coach is not able to be humorous, or if he is so emotionally involved that he is unable to provide the necessary release, he may anticipate his inadequacy and focus attention upon someone who can be humorous. An assistant coach, the team comedian, a yell-leader, a spectator, someone on the other team, or even an inanimate object such as a piece of unusual equipment (jersey, shoe, facemask, etc.), or a physical facility (dressing room, bench, scoreboard, loudspeaker, etc.) can divert the players' attention and ease their anxiety.

Calm   Closely related to humor as a means of reducing anxiety is a calm demeanor by the coach during periods of great excitement. Bad breaks, bad calls by the official, momentum by the other team, and serious loss of effectiveness by players who are working hard can be demoralizing and destructive if the coach does not display to the athlete his feeling that the crisis will pass and that the situation presents no great problem.

The coach, quite obviously, can increase the excitement or frustration felt by the players by becoming excited and frustrated himself. There are times when this reaction may be natural and even necessary, but the coach must be careful to see to it that he does not add to the problems of the team by displaying a lack of control in periods that call for great emotional control and analytical thought.

Excitement   Excitement is very much a part of athletic contests. We have all witnessed it and felt it while watching athletes compete. For a player, the degree of excitement is likely to vary according to the importance of the game, the score, the crowd, and his own involvement.

As the season progresses and practice begins to become tedious, the coach can expect the early season excitement to wear off a little. On other occasions, particularly when preparing to play an opponent it can beat, the team may tend to relax mentally and become "flat." When a coach recognizes this feeling in his team, he may counter it, in part, with his own state of excitability. When this happens, the team members, witnessing the coach's excitement, are likely to begin to ask themselves, "What's going on here? Does he know something I don't know? Maybe I'd better shake myself a bit and keep pace with the guy!"

Coaches are rarely overconfident to the point of taking an opponent lightly. Generally, they feel that something is left undone and more work is needed. We have all seen enough upsets to know that this threat always hangs ominously over the heads of even the best teams. Yet, every team suffers the mental disease of flatness at some time during the season. Actually, the coach is making a subjective evaluation when he senses flatness in his team's efforts, but, as every coach will tell you, the periods are as obvious as the points on the scoreboard. The coach should make every effort to maintain the highest level of intensity possible in his athletes—excitement, well-timed, will help.

Anger   It is virtually impossible to avoid anger in athletics. A player or a coach invests too much of himself to avoid this emotion. The very nature of competition is such that failure and frustration are commonplace. A coach's anger is generally directed at a player in time of failure. Often, this anger takes on the form of punishment, but to be angry does not necessarily mean that the coach has to punish. There are two types of anger which coaches should examine very carefully to understand their value and effect on the team.

Negative Anger   To begin with, players often feel the need for punishment when they know they have done wrong or are playing badly. A good "chewing out," if it is not destructive, may be what is needed to snap a player out of an undesirable condition—he is "punished," accepts it, feels better, and goes out to perform in the manner expected of him. Negative anger, however, communicates to the player that he is a no good, worthless, incapable person. It is *destructive*. An emotional release for the coach is all that is accomplished. As for the player, it leads him to believe that he does not have it and that he is not worth the time the coach spends on him.

Positive Anger   This approach communicates that the coach has not even considered the player incapable of doing the job. It expresses his unhappiness with the *performance*, not the performer. A statement such as "You're the best lineman in the league. Now what the hell is going on? What's wrong? It's not like you!" is *constructive*. It lets the player know that the coach has the greatest amount of faith in him. He cares. He climbs inside the person and expresses, in essence, what the player himself feels.

Sarcasm   The use of sarcasm should be very limited, because it tends to make the player at whom it is directed resentful for long periods of time. Anger can be understood, accepted, and forgotten; sarcasm, because it is most often directed at a personality, cannot. Sarcasm has a terribly destructive effect on the suspicious athlete and must be avoided. It may, however, be used with the athlete who enjoys a humorous verbal battle—one who likes to use sarcasm himself in a friendly way.

COMMUNICATING WITH THE INDIVIDUAL

Successful communication is based on a combination of knowledge and respect for the person with whom the coach is communicating, in addition to the proper use of the skills of communication. Ineffective communication may not be the result of a lack of intelligence or a sincere interest in the person, but only a lack of skill in the art of communicating.

Essentially, the foundation of all communication is mutual respect and trust. Admittedly, if these feelings do not exist, effective communication may be difficult. Communication with others in the same manner as we would have them communicate with us may sound trite, but the gold in that rule has never lost its luster. The following principles are of value in conveying mutual respect and trust:

Create an atmosphere in which the player feels he has the right and the freedom to express his ideas. Make him know that his opinion counts. The manner and the personality of the coach will determine the method of doing this. His opinion may be stated openly, or it may be suggested subtly. This principle will conflict with the personal philosophy of some coaches who feel that it *is* the role of the player to accept without question the dictates of the coach, who not only has the right, but also the obligation to unequivocally demand strict adherence to his rules. For harmony to exist on a team, "communication" should not become "dictation." Many players will submit totally to the will of the coach without question and will appear to be happily adjusted and secure in the subjugation. Total submission to a strong will results in an "incomplete" player— one who is deficient in initiative and leadership. Communication is a *two-way* street.

When an athlete fails, statements of understanding should precede criticism or instruction.   Failure in athletics is obvious to most people, particularly to the performer. He does not need additional attention focused on the act by a coach intent on "coaching." For example, a coach witnesses his player's failure to stop a high scorer from another team. He should use an approach like, "Boy, that guy was unconscious! Everything he threw went in. I thought you did a good job, but there was no stopping him tonight! We'll get him next time!" (followed later, of course, by the corrections you feel are necessary after his confidence has been restored), as opposed to, "Nice job, Anderson! You really did a job on him. My mother could have done better than you!" which does nothing but add humiliation to the pain of failure.

Praise achievements or efforts—not personality.   Praise for the individual personality can be frightening, because it suggests that the coach's admiration for the person is dependent upon the success of his play. An outstanding performance or a miserable performance should not change the coach's opinion of his player's character. The same, of course, is true for the use of criticism.

Avoid the "I told you so!" routine.   The coach who makes himself superior to the situation may quickly lose rapport with the player. It is really amazing how many coaches try to absolve themselves of blame for failure by saying something like, "I *told* those guys what to do and they didn't do it." Weak coaches "tell" players; great coaches build habits through hours of work and then "remind" players. Weak coaches escape responsibility; great coaches assume it and go to work.

Remember the simple idea that people resent being criticized, preached at, and talked to.   Many coaches are guilty of overcoaching. Criticism or repeated instruction may enforce the inadequacy in the athlete. If the coach tells him enough times that he is poor, he will be poor. In a great majority of cases the athlete's performance would increase in efficiency if the coach played up the athlete's positive skills and *ignored* the errors.

Consider the value of inserting "personal" touches and references. Adjustments in the communication process must be made to fit the diversity of interests, needs, and capacities of the individuals. Before the coach can do this with full effectiveness, he must know as much as possible about each athlete. One procedure for doing this is to have each athlete fill out a personal profile sheet early in the season. This will enable the coach to become better acquainted with the athlete's background. The coach can refer to the sheet in his free time or when the need arises. Figures 2 and 3 are samples of personal data sheets which may be used by the coach.

The player profile should be considered a guide by the coach. If there are any additional materials he feels are important, they should be included. Any information which the coach feels will help him understand the athlete better should be part of the player profile sheet. The aim of the information is to aid the coach in better understanding the athlete and to have a greater feeling for his players as individuals and the team as a whole.

The coach should keep in mind that some athletes are sensitive to filling out forms that ask for personal information. The athlete may fear that the personal information will be used to hurt him in some way, particularly the suspicious athlete. The coach should be aware of this fear. The athlete must be assured that the information aids the coach in handling him more effectively by enabling the coach to become personally acquainted with him. He must do everything possible to assure the athlete that the information will not be used against him or to hurt him in any way. If the coach does not keep the information confidential, he will not be trusted. If the coach guards against the information being used in a destructive manner by anyone, the player will have confidence in him.

FIGURE 2. Player Profile of Player A—Basketball

Name: Richard Jones

Age: 16   Birthdate: January 5, 1950   Grade: Junior

Home Address: 127 Crescent Way, San Jose   Phone: 279-8316

Father's Name: Charles E. Jones

Mother's Name: Sarah Bennings Jones

Father's Occupation-Position: Lawyer

Mother's Occupation-Position: High School English Teacher

Siblings, Names & Ages: None

Educational/Occupational Goals: Accountant

Weekly Income/Allowance: $10.00 weekly allowance

Girlfriend's Name: Alice Smith   Favorite Sport: Basketball

School Grades by Subject: Math-A, English-A, Physics-A,

   History-B, Chemistry-B

Extra Curricular Activities in School: Journalism Club, Student

   Council, Chess Club

Offices Held in Clubs or Activities: President-Student Council,

   Treasurer-Journalism Club

Hobbies: Sports Cars, Chess, Reads

Why Participating: To get a letter (school)

Sports Heroes: John Brodie   Roberto Clemente

Favorite School Subject: Math, Chemistry

Favorite Teacher: Mr. Black   Religion: Methodist

What Sports Did Father Play: Basketball, baseball

Coach's Personal Note: Popular boy in his class and in school

---

Summary and Evaluation of Player Profiles

Player A appears to be a boy from a middle class family who is quite active in school. He has many interests and activities and gets around a great deal. He comes from a more sophisticated family and appears to have a more independent background than player B. He is less inclined to make sports the sole part of his life. He may be less dedicated than others because of the diversity in his life. If he is dedicated, he would be a good leader because of his experience.

FIGURE 3. Player Profile of Player B—Basketball

Name: Juan Lopez

Age: 16   Birthdate: August 8, 1950   Grade: Junior

Home Address: 1842 Guadalupe Way, East S.J.   Phone: none

Father's Name: Hector Lopez

Mother's Name: Camilia Lopez

Father's Occupation-Position: Laborer

Mother's Occupation-Position: Housewife

Siblings, Names & Ages: Al-20, Carmen-18, Jesus-14, Maria-9

Educational/Occupational Goals: Crane Operator

Weekly Income/Allowance: Part time grocery clerk-$8.00 week

Girlfriend's Name: none   Favorite Sport: Basketball, baseball

School Grades by Subject: Math-C, English-C, Physics-C,

History-B, Wood Shop-A

Extra Curricular Activities in School: none

Offices Held in Clubs or Activities: none

Hobbies: Sports-football, baseball

Why Participating: Wanted to play

Sports Heroes: O. J. Simpson, Juan Marichal, Willie Mays, Bill

Russell

Favorite School Subject: Wood Shop

Favorite Teacher: Mr. Alvarez   Religion: Catholic

What Sports Did Father Play: Basketball, football, baseball

Coach's Personal Note: Shy, withdrawn, always playing ball or

practicing; usually talking about or participating in some type of

athletics.

Player B is withdrawn from the mainstream in school. He is from a minority group, a member of a large family, a hard worker and less inclined to have the benefits of a middle class family. He seems dedicated to athletics and uses this as an outlet in his life.

The coach may be able to get a different feel for the backgrounds of the two athletes. Player A may be easier for the coach to understand and deal with because their backgrounds may be similar. He can better sense how to handle him. With Player B, he will need to get a better understanding of his cultural background, and it will take longer to understand how to motivate him. Whereas Player A should be easier to become acquainted with, Player B will need more concern and understanding from the coach if he is to be motivated on the basis of his needs.

COMMUNICATION WITH A TEAM

A great deal of the coach's time is taken in discussing problems with the entire team. Just as each individual is unique, each team is unique. The team's character changes as the athletes change, since the team is simply a composite of all of the characteristics of each team member. If the coach knows the characteristics of the team members, he has a good "feel" for what his team is like as a "whole." This should govern his approach to the team.

Understand the common needs shared by all members of a team. The team is composed of individuals with certain needs. If the majority of these individuals have a particular need or exhibit a common personality trait, then that need or trait depicts that team. The coach must then keep in mind the particular type of team he is working with and adjust to them just as he would adjust his attack to fit a team that is slow, or to a team that is small, or to a team that is quick. With regard to size and ability, a coach takes advantage of the strength he has on his team and compensates for the weaknesses. He must make the same adjustments with personality types. For example, a "tough" team would be handled much differently from a "tender" team. If the tough team is treated like little kids, the coach may lose them, whereas he might reach the tender ones. By the same token, if the coach chews out the tough ones, they will respond well, but the tender team would fold.

A coach may have a wide variety of team types. He may have a club that is rebellious, or one that is unstable, or one that is not particularly bright. He must keep in mind, when dealing with his unit, which approach is best with the personality traits that are strong. If they are aggressive, develop that; if tough, develop that; if the team is bright, develop that, and so on.

Of course, all players will not belong to one type, but generally a team can be categorized according to the majority of types present. With the "sensitive" team, the coach should direct his attack at the tough athlete. He can take it. The coach should not forget to compensate for the player's toughness in some way, or otherwise he will wonder why he is the one always being chewed out. The coach may tell him the reason for this behind closed doors, "I know I've been getting on your back a lot lately and I want you to know my reasons for doing it. It's because you're one of my tougher players—one of the few who can take a chewing out. I'm directing my comments at you because I know you can take it. Through you I'm really talking to the rest of the team, but I'm afraid to single out any one of the other players, because he might be destroyed by the criticism. I know you won't be."

A coach can employ the same kinds of techniques in communicating with a team as he would in communicating with a player. To deal with problem teams, refer to the chart on recommended procedures for communicating with problem athletes mentioned earlier in this chapter.

Provide the team with some information to help them understand the coach as a human being. At the beginning of the season it may be wise for the coach to mention a few facts about himself to let the players know what to expect. For example, "It's my nature to be a demanding person, and because of this there are times when you're really going to hate me, but one of my aims is to have a team that's well conditioned, and so I'm going to see to it that all of you are in shape. You may not agree with this, but it's my philosophy. I'm a hard working person myself and I expect the same out of you."

The coach may have to repeat this and other basic information occasionally to explain his moods and his frustrations, particularly when he has lost his temper or, in some way, behaved badly. Comments such as "I have my feelings too, and this season is just as hard on me as it is on you. Every once in a while my temper may get the best of me and I may chew on somebody, as I did yesterday, but please try to remember that this season is just as important to me as it is to you," will go a long way toward making the players appreciate the coach's position and toward understanding him as a human being.

The more open and honest the coach becomes about himself, the closer the players will feel toward him. This leads to some problems, but it can also lead to some advantages.

Players "need" the coach after a loss. Players can take care of themselves very nicely after a win, but the one time they really need a coach is after a loss. At this time, the coach's behavior is really quite critical.

The first thing the coach should do after losing is to quickly, but carefully, explore his feelings about the loss. If he is angry with the team and moved to punish them, he should do his best to curb the emotion and keep his mouth shut. The team members are already "down" in this situation. They have been hurt badly enough as it is. There is no value in, or reason for, increasing the pain felt. This is the time for the coach to be emotionally stable and to provide support. In particular, he needs to support those who have worked hard and done their best. For those who did not produce, this is not the time to punish them. The coach can let them know later by means of films, or statistics, or through personal conversation. Now, however, he should just ignore them. If, however, the coach realizes he is too angry and he cannot handle the anger, it is best that he be straight and honest with his feelings. One way is to have a team meeting immediately after the game during which he expresses his angry feelings. It is important to remember that this is being done to help the coach deal with his feelings, and it is not to be interpreted as only a means of punishing the team. To do this properly can have some benefits. For one thing, it helps the coach relieve himself of the pent up emotions that might otherwise bother him later.

Coaches who hold their feelings inside often take out their anger later in a more destructive way. It may come out in the form of snide remarks, sarcasm, or insults. This is far more destructive in the long run than the coach exploding after a game. A second advantage is that the team will become more aware that the coach has some genuine concern for the team and the game. A coach who does not explode when the team feels he should, or when they feel they have it coming, may begin to feel that the coach does not care, or that he has given up on them. By expressing the pent up emotion, he lets them know otherwise. It is wise for the coach to remind them that he is mad, because they are capable of performing better, and that he, personally, is angry *for* them, because he knows they can excel. In this way, they will feel supported.

The coach must be careful not to let his anger be destructive. To humiliate a player, or to blame an athlete for the loss of a game, may lose a player for a career. If the coach is angry at one player only, he should talk to him alone rather than take out his feelings on the entire team. If the coach takes it out on one player in front of the team, both the team member and the team may turn against the coach, because he was excessively abusive to the individual. If the coach realizes that the reason for "blowing his top" is to get rid of his own anger and to spark the team, his approach will be more productive than destructive in the long run.

View films "positively." When done properly, there is no better method for players to learn than that of viewing films taken of games or practices. The movie can really tell a story—often an embarrassing one for the players. The visual proof of success or failure provides the coach with objective evidence of the team's efficiency. It is a rare occasion when a coach is pleased after viewing a film. The very act of viewing tends to become a *search for errors.* There is nothing wrong with that in itself, but when it comes time to show the film to the team, often an attitude on the part of the coach that was once analytical and detached becomes critical and personal. At this time the coach tends to violate many of the "rules" mentioned in the section on communicating with an individual: he criticizes or corrects without understanding the failure; he assumes the supercilious air of an "I told you so" critic who is safely out of the picture and not subject to scrutiny; and he fills the viewing period with sarcasm and spite.

Corrections must be made of course. The manner in which this is done, however, is important. Again, to berate players and to focus on their failures is of little value. Rather than saying, "Look how you missed that block, Walker! The whole play is ruined because of your lousy effort," a coach may say, "Look at what would happen here if we get a block. We'd go all the way. Campbell does a great job of busting the tackle." If the player has been well coached, he very likely is aware of the mistake. Mention of his inadequacy should take place only in private.

When the film shows a player making a serious mistake, it is best for the coach to show the player another example of his own play when he is doing the job correctly and to say something like, "You missed it before, but watch the job you do this time. You do it beautifully here. Do you see the difference between this and the first time?" The coach should not compare a poor performance of one player with a good performance of another. If, by chance, the coach is dealing with a very sensitive person, he should point out only the successful effort.

A very effective system to follow in viewing films is to have the individual player rate his own performance on each play. Using a performance evaluation card (Figure 4) may help him.

After viewing the play three or four times, the player would rate himself and give his reason for success or failure. The coach also rates each player's efficiency on every play and matches his ratings with those of the players to see if the athlete really understands the difference between a good job and a poor one. If the evaluations and the reasons for failure are nearly identical, little needs to be said. If, however, there is a great difference in the ratings, additional instruction must be given the player when time per-

FIGURE 4. Performance Evaluation Card

	Play number
Excellent _____	
Good _____	
Fair _____	
Poor _____	
Reason for success or failure:	

mits. Comparing the coach's and player's evaluation cards is an excellent form of communication. It causes little or no embarrassment, because the problem is not discussed before the group, and the player's concentration on his own skills is enhanced, because he is evaluating rather than hiding from himself.

During a game, limit the information, keep it simple, and make sure the players hear it. One basketball coach tells the story of how he confirmed his suspicion that it was somewhat pointless for him to talk to his players during a tension-packed game, because they simply did not hear what he had to say. As an experiment, during a time out in one particularly tense period of a game, and while the spectators were noisily displaying their excitement and enthusiasm, the coach merely moved his lips without emitting a sound. To his audible question, "Do you understand?" the players confidently nodded "Yes!" and went back on the court.

While the story is true, the principle may be stretched a bit. Players *do* hear and respond, of course, but probably not to the degree the coach would like to think. How many times has a coach seen players run right out on the court or field and do exactly the *opposite* of what he asked? The point here is that the coach should *limit* the information he is trying to communicate, keep it *simple*, and make certain that the players really hear him. This is particularly true in crucial and exciting games—the ones in which a coach feels the need to convey a great deal of complex information. It is best to talk about only *one* thing to a team during a time out. The coach should make it a *review* of an idea discussed prior to the game (not some new principle introduced for the first time), and should ask certain people, about whom he may have doubts, to repeat the information.

RECOGNIZING COMMUNICATION GAPS

Effective coaching is largely dependent upon the degree of player receptiveness. Many things can happen during a season to cause a communication gap between a player and his coach. It is important that the coach recognize these problems and overcome them as early as possible. Essentially, an athlete wants to feel respected and appreciated. If, for any reason, he does not have this feeling, problems are bound to arise.

Because the coach represents authority, some players may be fearful of him and are reluctant to "open up" in his presence. This is a somewhat normal reaction, especially with younger players, and does not represent a serious threat to successful communication. The serious communication gaps are most often the result of conflicting philosophies or clashing personalities. But, large or small, a communication gap is usually the result of a person's being afraid to tell another how he feels. On occasion, the coach may be completely unaware that the gap exists, but if he is sensitive and alert, he will be able to discern a verbal or behavioral difference in the player, which indicates its existence.

Verbal The verbal clues may come from a wide variety of sources. The coach receives reports that his players feel differently from what he had believed. These reports may say things in a newspaper, T.V., or radio interview which are surprising. Another indication is the player's reluctance to communicate—he withdraws, avoids the coach on and off the field, or stops talking even to others when the coach comes near his group.

Behavioral There are certain body movements which also may indicate the presence of a communication blockage. Crossing the arms in front, drawing an imaginary line with his foot between the coach and himself, looking down or away when the coach is talking are a few of the obvious examples.

Some coaches will always have this gap. They are just not comfortable with their players, and they accept the fact by saying, "Well, that's just the way I am." Communication can be improved if coaches will follow these suggestions:

1. The most effective communication takes place in a one-to-one situation—when the player is responsible for responding totally to the coach. The poorest communication takes place when there are all kinds of external stimuli impinging upon the player (at practices with spectators watching or other players engaged in activity). The coach, therefore, must be extremely brief when communicating with the group under these conditions.
2. The time when players are least ready to communicate is after they have committed an error. Most people are on guard when they have done something wrong. If the coach tries to communicate at this time, he may find the player blocking him out completely, misinterpreting intentionally, or being openly hostile.
3. The coach should make an attempt to remove the behavioral manifestations of communication blockage such as uncrossing the player's arms when talking to him, getting the player to look at him, or stopping him from doodling with his feet. He should either stop the player from doing these things or he should not attempt to communicate at that time.
4. A player should be made to feel that he has the freedom to let the coach know how he feels without being penal-

ized. If the coach recognizes the existence of a gap, it is best that he approach the player and, behind closed doors, ask directly that the barriers be removed. If the gap is a result of differences of opinion over decisions, strategy, or philosophy, then the coach should make an effort to further justify his position. The player can then be given an opportunity to make his feelings known. Just because the coach *listens* to the player does not mean that he has to *do* what he asks. The most secure coaches will not be threatened by this situation. The insecure coaches will be, because they are afraid that they may be shown to be wrong or that their authority is being questioned.

5. Finally, a very effective technique for eliminating communication gaps is to give the player (or players) the opportunity to try the thing he really believes in. Flexibility on the part of the coach in allowing a stubborn player to find out for himself will both gain him the player's respect and probably convince the player that the coach was right. (The assumption made here is that the coach is the expert and *is* right—it is his business, and he is in a much better position to judge than the player.) Once the player has tried and failed, he will more readily accept the future wishes of the coach. If the player was right, the coach should recognize this and use the player's new and more effective approach.

By adjusting the methods of communication to fit the different needs of the various personality types, the coach can achieve enormously rewarding results and help to enhance his team's chances for success.

chapter 6
TEAM COHESION

The term "teamwork" universally connotes cooperation on the part of a number of individuals working toward a common goal. Cooperation exists in all walks of life and is an integral part of every success story. The astronauts' conquest of space was the product of a very extensive *team* effort; a motion picture is produced only through the special *cooperative* talents of a great many people; an automobile is assembled by many men who perform special and *coordinated* tasks. The list of examples, of course, is endless, but the real value and importance of collective efficiency is most meaningful in the activity which engendered the term teamwork—*competitive athletics.*

Perhaps the greatest reward to be derived from membership on a team is the development of lasting friendships. These friendships are the natural result of the interaction taking place within a team composed of individuals unselfishly helping each other accomplish personal goals designed to enhance the total team picture.

The development of team cohesion is one of the most difficult tasks facing a coach. He must first have players available who are willing to *sacrifice, cooperate,* and *work hard,* even though only a few can play and really represent the team. Underlying this feeling of cooperativeness and sacrifice is an intense rivalry for a position on the team. This rivalry exists long before an opponent is encountered, and it continues throughout the duration of the season. If the subs honestly pull for the regulars and, at the same time, feel that they are getting a fair shake from the coach, team cohesion results, and the coach has done a masterful job. If, however, the players on the bench secretly hope that the regulars will fail, or if they feel that the players on the field should not be there at all, the coach is faced with a serious problem. To have a truly cohesive group, each individual must be willing to lose himself within the group, not to the degree of being satisfied with being a second-stringer, but to the degree of placing the welfare of the team ahead of his own personal goals. He can continue to work diligently toward his goal of becoming a first stringer but not at the expense of the team, and he should not have a feeling of animosity if he fails to achieve his personal goal.

Before true team cohesion can exist, these conditions should prevail:

Mutual respect   The players and the coach must appreciate the value of each individual to the team. This can be accomplished only after each player understands the difficulty of the other positions of play.

Effective communication   Each team member must be willing to communicate and work toward understanding others, as well as helping others to understand him. Since communication is a two-way street, it must begin with the efforts of each player.

A feeling of importance   The genuine feeling that the athlete is a member of the team and that his feelings are being considered must be present. He should know that he will be recognized for whatever sacrifice he makes and be supported by the other players and the coach.

4 *Common goals* There should be a common belief in, or an acceptance of, the team philosophy and the plans they must follow to achieve their goals.

5 *Fair treatment* Every player needs to feel that he is being treated as fairly as possible and that he is being given an opportunity to display and develop his talents to the maximum. Every player needs to feel that he is being given an equal shot at the first team and that he is being provided with a fair opportunity to play when the situation presents itself.

DEVELOPING AN IMAGE

In general, people react on the basis of how they view both themselves and others. In athletics, the image players have of their opponent and the confidence they have in themselves play a tremendously important part in the degree of success they will achieve. The variety of attitudes creating images should be considered in evaluating any situation:

What you think of yourself This will vary from player to player, but there is usually a consensus of agreement about *team* characteristics. Athletes create an image of themselves as an aggressive team or as a timid team, a tough team or an easy team, a team that comes from behind to win in the fourth quarter or a team that fades early, an ambitious team or a lazy team. A team usually functions within the image it has of itself. In psychology this is known as the "self-fulfilling prophesy." That is, people have a tendency to do those things they already believe about themselves. For example, a team that thinks it is hard working is probably a team that will work hard; a team that thinks it is lacking in confidence probably lacks confidence; and a team that thinks it is aggressive, very likely will be. Simply stated, people react on the basis of how they feel about themselves.

Knowing how the other team views itself can often have an effect on how the coach might prepare to face them. For example, he knows they view themselves as tough, and this should have some effect on his preparation and should guide him in the development of his strategy.

What the other team thinks of you   What the other team thinks of you is very important. They may be intimidated by you or they may see you as no challenge. The image they have of you often determines their style of play, their degree of involvement, and their determination to win.

When a coach's perceptions about the other team are accurate, he is likely to have a game plan in line with what should be taking place. If, for example, he knows that his team must be tough in the fourth quarter because that is when the other team comes on particularly strong, and he prepares his team for it physically and psychologically, it may make a big difference. If the coach is able to discern a weakness in another team and is able to take advantage of that weakness, his team's gains may be great. By the same token, if the coach's evaluation is wrong and the other team is not what he expects them to be, the psychological shock may be great. If teams are more than what the coach sees them as being, his team's preparation will not be what it should be and the possibility of an upset is great.

What you think the other team thinks of you   What you believe to be the other team's image of you and what it actually is may be two entirely different things. An opponent can be "mis-read." Most athletes have been beaten badly or embarrassed by a younger and less experienced player whom they thought had a very healthy respect for them and whom they knew would not dare challenge the supremacy of the old master.

Intimidation or overconfidence may be the result of an incorrect estimate. For example, a team may feel they have a reputation for being very aggressive and as a result, a less talented opponent will react timidly. For a team to assume what another team thinks is poor strategy. In the long run, the team can only depend upon its own personal image.

What you and the other team actually are   Different from the first three images, perhaps, is what a team *actually* is. This is often determined by the view of a third party or by very objective direct evaluation of various aspects of the game. Often coaches base their opinion of the team not on what it actually is, but on what it potentially could be.

Positive Image

To maintain a positive image, a team must continue to act in an exemplary fashion. A negative image can result from one mistake or from one indiscretion. Generally, the players feel positively toward their own team. In almost all cases, they feel that they are right and that the other team is wrong. Given the choice, they would choose to remain with the players with whom they have gone through a lot of suffering. A team with a positive image usually will appear congenial and will seem as though they work well together. The team with the positive image has cohesion. The following are factors responsible for the development of a positive image:

1. *Winning*   A winning team is more likely to have a positive image than a losing team. A winning team's actions or behavior is viewed as good solely because they are winning. What they do is considered positive. They may be *doing* the same thing they have been doing for years, but when they win, their actions are considered positive simply because they are now winning. This is known as the "halo effect." That is, if a team wins, they are good. Whatever they are doing is good, and whatever they are practicing is good.

Discipline   The positive image often grows out of being disciplined and a negative image grows out of being undisciplined. Orderliness, as opposed to slovenliness, is necessary for a positive image.

3 *Strength of the coach*   The ethical values of the coach are of major importance. If he is seen as a gentleman—one who is moral and ethical—and if his behavior is exemplary outside the sports environment, the players are much more likely to have an ethically positive image. To maintain his positive image, the coach must take action with rule-breakers. The players should expect to be suspended for breaking the established rules.

4 *Sub-culture*   In certain schools there is a traditional expectation that the players will behave or perform in a certain way, and if they do not conform to the ethics of this sub-culture, they will either be ostracized or dropped completely from the group.

Negative Image

This image presents an individual athlete or a team as being either socially unacceptable or as using unethical techniques. You often hear them referred to as a "dirty club." The team thus labeled is not prone to think ill of itself, however. It is difficult for people to view themselves negatively. Often rationalization is offered to justify what is being done, "It was their fault that I did that. I punched the guy in the mouth because he was asking for it. He started it!" People tend only to view others negatively. There is an exception to this. It is very possible that an athlete may view himself negatively from a success point of view. "I'm just not a good player. I don't deserve to play." The player thinks of himself as a loser. It is much more difficult for a player to change his negative success-image, than it is for him to change his ethical image. The following are factors responsible for a negative image:

Sub-culture   Certain teams or certain players come from an area in which an image exists purely on the basis of the sub-culture. Again, this is an example of the self-fulfilling prophesy. If a player feels that he has an area of inadequacy, then he will probably have such an area. Certain sub-cultures in our society learn quite early to limit their expectations and think less of themselves, because it is how they are viewed by others, or it is how they think they are viewed by others.

Broken rules   Lack of adherence to rules of good conduct is very destructive to the team image. A negative image usually starts from the way rules are broken, and they are often broken in anger. One fight can lead to a bad image. In viewing a film of an opponent, if he does one dirty thing, he is, from that time on, a dirty player. When the player views the same act committed by himself, he has the tendency to convert it into something positive, "We are just hard hitters!"

Coach's personality   Players are prone to be very much like their coach or are selected by him because they are similar to him. If the coach's image is negative, there is a good chance that the team's image will be negative also.

Reputation   Some teams feel they must perpetuate a bad image, because it is the mark of their school or organization. It provides them with a type of "in-group." It may take a concerted, all-out effort over a period of time to eliminate such an image.

CHANGING AN IMAGE EXTERNALLY

Uniforms or uniform colors   A colorless or unenthusiastic team can give itself some fire and can help to change its image by changing uniforms. This may not be easy, because it involves the changing of a tradition. When such changes are made, considerable dissatisfaction may occur among those who do not like change. When a team breaks a longstanding tradition by dramatically changing their uniform, they may receive criticism from the public. In time, however, changes are accepted.

Mascot   A mascot can reflect how a team feels about itself. A change of mascot may make a difference in the image a team has of itself or in the image it presents to the public. For example, if it is possible, a team might change its image from a small, quick team (symbolized by an eagle) to a big, over-powering club (symbolized by a lion).

Team slogans   The adoption or change of certain slogans may help to keep before the players and the fans a set of new ideals or goals. "Three yards and a cloud of dust," "The Runnin Redskins," "Come inside our twenty and bleed," and "Show me a good loser and I'll show you a loser" are a few of many examples.

Formations or rituals   A pre-game warm-up activity may be devised to display the special talents of a particular team and thereby help that team gain a certain psychological advantage. A great deal of intimidation may take place before the contest actually begins. Against some teams, a spirited, aggressive, and ferocious pre-game warm-up may be effective, while against others the best approach may be one of almost total unconcern. The key to the effectiveness of the activity lies in the interest shown by the athletes on the other team. To illustrate, the players on a basketball team may be watching the players on the other team easily stuff the ball; other jumpers may be watching the casual way the favorite goes about warming up; or a baseball team may be standing in the dugout watching the other team hitting the ball out of the park in batting practice.

Change opponents when necessary   Players may have an image of opponents that the coach feels is undesirable. It just may be that this opponent should be avoided, if possible, or at least scheduled during a part of the season in which a loss to the team will not be so destructive to the image the coach is trying to create. Perhaps another opponent may be substituted to help the coach develop a certain psychological trait that he feels is essential to the success of his team.

CHANGING AN IMAGE INTERNALLY

Internal changes occur much more gradually and take much more effort to develop. The personality of the coach and of the athlete will determine the approach to be taken. An excellent method for eliciting player attitudes about desirable images is to simply have the players list the teams and the players they admire most, and then have them state the reasons for their feelings. The coach also may ask the players to describe their own image as they see it. In a follow up discussion, the players may be told of the results of the survey and have the question put to them, "Would you really like to be like this team (or player, if this is the case)? If so, how do we go about getting it?" From this, the goals and the schedules may be formulated and the work begun. Figure 5 is a sample form the player may use to evaluate his own and his opponent's image.

DEVELOPING COHESION

Cohesion is at the core of most outstanding teams. Although there may be numerous definitions of team cohesion, each of which would be correct for our purpose, we may define it as a group of individuals thinking, feeling, and acting as a single unit. It is the ability for individuals to make an emotional investment in a group and believe that the outcome of the unit's effort is more important than the outcome of any individual's personal effort. Such a unit becomes a self-disciplining, autonomously-functioning group. Each member becomes responsible not only for his behavior, but also for the behavior of the other members of that unit.

The members of a cohesive team do not have to second guess other team members. They do not have to wonder what they might do—they know what they will do. This saves time, effort, and above all costly errors particularly during crucial periods. As one athlete describes cohesion,

FIGURE 5. Image Evaluation Card

```
┌─────────────────────────────────────────────────────────────┐
│                                                               │
│                        Name _____         │
│                                                               │
│      Teams you most admire:        Reason:                    │
│                                                               │
│      1. _____           _____   │
│                                                               │
│      2. _____           _____   │
│                                                               │
│      3. _____           _____   │
│                                                               │
│      4. _____           _____   │
│                                                               │
│                                                               │
│      Players you most admire:      Reason:                    │
│                                                               │
│      1. _____           _____   │
│                                                               │
│      2. _____           _____   │
│                                                               │
│      3. _____           _____   │
│                                                               │
│      4. _____           _____   │
│                                                               │
│                                                               │
│      Briefly describe the type of athlete you are. What do you think are │
│      the major strengths and weaknesses of this type?         │
│                                                               │
│                                                               │
└─────────────────────────────────────────────────────────────┘
```

"It is like one's body—the eye will see it and the hand reacts. They work in perfect harmony together. The eye doesn't have to wonder what the hand will do. It knows."

In attempting to develop team cohesion, it is recommended that consideration be given to the following ideas:

Have the players become acquainted with the responsibilities of others. There is no more effective way for an athlete to develop an appreciation for the job being done by someone else then to get in and do the job himself. Players should be given the opportunity to play other positions and change roles. They will both learn a new respect for that job, and they will go back to their old positions with an added incentive. Recognition of the contributions of others is essential to strong team unity. On many professional football teams, it is becoming the thing to do for the quarterback to take the pass-protection blockers out to dinner after a victory. He knows how little publicity they receive and how important they are to him. It is his way of saying to them, "The people up there may not understand the importance of your role, but I know and I say, thanks!"

Have the players observe and record the efforts of other athletes at their position. Closely associated with the idea of becoming acquainted with the other positions is the utilization of substitute athletes as observers of the effectiveness of the play of others. They may do this in a variety of ways: keeping statistics, recording the reactions of an opponent, or observing the fine points of play for sake of analysis. It gives the player a responsibility and helps make him feel a part of the team even though he has been relegated to the role of substitute.

Know something personal about each player. The coach's knowledge of the player's personality and background will help make a more cohesive group. The recognition of what is important to others (a girlfriend, a birthday, future ambitions, etc.) has a profound effect on the cooperativeness and congeniality of the group.

Develop pride within the sub-units and recognize them for their special contributions. Within a team there are subgroups that work together as cohesive units in a very specialized way. In football, the backs work separately from the line; in basketball, back-court men work to perfect skills different from those needed by the forwards and centers; in baseball, the pitchers follow an independent program of conditioning and training different from that of the rest of the team. This separation of the sub-units may be further broken down in most cases (offensive line—defensive line, centers—guards, etc.), and, with this further breakdown, the development of a stronger comradeship may take place among those players who make up the unit. Competition between sub-units (offense vs. defense for example) not only may lead to the development of stronger skills on the part of both groups, but also may create in the players a highly developed sense of pride in the specialized role they play. The pride that exists within a sub-unit is likely to become an integral part of the entire team's pride when an opponent is met. All members look to that sub-unit with the confidence that they can do their job in actual competition as well as in practice. One of the most obvious examples of cohesiveness is when players at the sidelines empathize with and enthusiastically support the members of a specialized sub-group. The coach must recognize special efforts or talents and compliment the players both publicly and privately.

Allow representatives from each sub-group to meet regularly with the coach. Each sub-group should be represented in meetings with the coach, first as a means of recognizing that specialized group, and second, as a means of making known the needs and feelings of that group. The meetings can be used to develop better communication by discussing team problems, and how they may be solved. It may be used to discuss the general attitude of the team, and what the players feel is necessary to become more successful.

Have team members feel that they are a part of the team; make them know that their voice will be heard. If there is to be cohesion, the feeling "Why should I say anything? He never listens to me anyway" must never develop. The kind of cohesion that is really important is the kind that includes the *whole* group. Cohesion must include *all* members. In order to develop cohesion and communication, some coaches have an "open door" policy. Any player may speak to the coach in private. They are assured by the coach that their comments will be made in complete privacy and never go beyond the coach.

Set goals and take pride in their accomplishment. A team must know where it is going. Players should try to set attainable goals so that a feeling of success can be achieved. Success is of tremendous importance in the development of team pride. Goals may be set individually as well as collectively. To develop further cohesion, the goals may be discussed individually with each player and eventually with the team. Using this approach, the athlete can feel he has participated in setting his own goals and, by so doing, becomes more responsible. As an example, a data sheet (Figure 6) might be used by a basketball player in determining his goals. By having goals, the athlete knows where he is

FIGURE 6. Goal Achievement Card

	Last Year	This Year	What you feel would be outstanding year
Name			
Position			
F.G.A.			
F.G. Made			
Pct.			
F.T.A.			
F.T. Made			
Pct.			
Rebounds			
Defensive Ave.			
Assists			
Turnovers			

headed and what is expected of him. Moreover, he feels more a part of the team when he accomplishes his goals.

Allow players to know their status on the team and provide a justification for that status. Each player must feel that he has had an equal chance to make the team. If a player can be shown statistically why he is not playing, he can accept his role. If possible, it is best to present to the player objective evidence of his position on the team so that the coach's decision is not put on a personal basis. Then, definite goals can be set up toward which the player can work. If a player can be shown where he is deficient, as well as the methods necessary to overcome his weaknesses, he can then genuinely, and with appreciation, understand his position and the position of others who are playing. He will both appreciate and support the other members of the team.

Emphasize the value of discipline. Adherence to rules designed to help a team reach its goals can become one of the central cohesive forces on the team. Real pride often results from a group of players sharing a difficult situation. A very demanding coach who unmercifully drives his players may unconsciously create a strong cohesiveness between the players who share the adversity. The more severe the strain and the misery that the players successfully survive, the closer they may become. The most cohesive unit is made up of men who have gone through a battle together. The greater the potential danger, the more cohesive the group. Discipline is also necessary for team cohesion. Most games involve a large number of rules and a large number of technicalities. The more disciplined the team, the better able they will be to handle the situation.

SUB-UNIT COHESION

Sub-unit cohesion is a formation composed of two or more players whose philosophy, behavior, or verbalizations are different from the basic aims, goals, or philosophy of the other players or the coach. Sub-unit cohesion may be either positive or negative.

Positive Unit Cohesion

A team may be divided into a number of sub-units, each building its own esprit-de-corps, its own goals, and its own ideals—all adding to the total team picture. For example, an offensive backfield or a defensive line may take great pride in what they do, and through their special efforts, the success of the overall team is greatly increased. They may give themselves a special name like the "Crushers" or the "Destroyers." The name describes the unit's pride and goals.

When all sub-units are producing effectively, a great team results. Antagonism may occur, however, if the sub-units do not work together productively. The coach, therefore, should be careful not to focus too much attention on one unit at the expense of another. One unit must not become dominant.

To develop positive team units, positive goals for the sub-unit must be created and the special achievements of that sub-unit must be recognized. The whole team can identify with the success of any sub-unit when it is obvious that the success of that sub-unit is adding to the effectiveness of the entire team.

Negative Team Cohesion

Negative attitudes result when a sub-unit is working against, or at least is not in unison with, the team. A clique develops. Its actions are rarely in the open; it acts subtly. A clique usually comes from some gap in communication or from some unfulfilled need and most definitely represents a lack of team cohesion. There are four major reasons why negative sub-units form:

Losing Cliques often result from losing. It takes great skill on the coach's part to keep a team cohesive when losing. One thing he can do is to point out from the loss what the team has learned and how this will help.

Players' needs not being met   A player may feel that he is not receiving the recognition he should be. This is not too difficult a problem to handle with the average athlete when it is discovered, but it may present a serious problem with the problem athletes. Cliques are usually caused by problem athletes. Their needs are difficult to meet. The con man, for example, is extremely self-centered and wants to fulfill his own needs totally. He goes about manipulating other people to do so. The non-coachable (rebellious) athlete is more open and direct in his efforts to undermine the team or the coach. It is easier to recognize this person. However, the coach may never be aware of the con man. He is much more subtle when he is undermining the team. As a matter of fact, the coach may be great friends with the con man, as, all the while, he is intent on splitting up the team.

Players not getting an opportunity to play   It is difficult for any player to sit on the bench. Not receiving the opportunity to play is one of the prime reasons for the development of team division. The coach can have his substitutes feel more a part of the team if they are assigned specific duties and get recognition for them. These duties might involve keeping track of an opponent to provide information to be used by the entire team. In any event, it helps a substitute feel more a part of the team and more a part of the action. Many teams have substitutes who have much less talent than the starting team, but who have a great deal of enthusiasm and spirit. If the coach can help develop this enthusiasm and spirit in some way, the entire team will benefit. On one football team, for example, the coach had his third string quarterback make an intense study of certain defensive backs in the first half. The coach would briefly consult with this player just before half time about any flaws he detected. Although the athlete was less talented, he was very bright and made several observations, which the coach used successfully. The athlete knew he was making a contribution and took pride in his accomplishments as much as if he were performing the act itself. The coach also recognized him for his contribution, making it even better.

One reason the coach must be aware of the needs of the substitutes is that a feeling of inadequacy often bothers them. The coach must express to each player his regard for him as a person and make him feel important. For example, one coach spent time with the substitutes alone, letting them know that he was fully aware of their feelings. He also expressed his appreciation and gratitude for their contributions, although they were not getting as much recognition as the regulars. He recognized the time and effort they put in and, for that reason, they were considered by him to be something special—a type of unsung hero. Substitutes who understand this can lend a great deal of support to the status of a team. An added benefit of this approach to substitutes is that they feel more confident when they do have the opportunity to play. They are apt to produce if their potential is continually encouraged. Moreover, the regulars will have greater faith in the substitutes if they do perform to their maximum. There is less chance that the gap between regulars and substitutes will cause a disruption in play.

The coach often responsible for cliques If the coach picks on a sub-unit and they retaliate, it may be the beginning of a problem. Some coaches actually create cliques, because they need something to use as a scapegoat. The coach does not play a group, they complain, and he uses them as the reason for the team's losing. Because of this "punishment" they become closer and, in so doing, are detrimental to team cohesion.

The coach may unconsciously create a clique by responding to a personal prejudice. He begins to isolate, negate, or push out of the main group the players who belong to the group against which he is prejudiced. As a result, they form a clique. They may be very subtly ostracized or simply not drawn into the mainstream of the team's activity. Whatever form the action takes, the result will be the same—the creation of a negative sub-unit.

HANDLING NEGATIVE SUB-UNITS

A coach must realize that the existence of a negative sub-unit will lead, in the long run, to the disruption of the team. For this reason, cliques must be broken up when they are recognized. When the group challenges the rules, the coach must, in turn, challenge the clique and re-emphasize the importance of adhering to the established rules. It is reasonable to say that the coach should listen to their gripes and respond to any legitimate complaints, but he cannot allow the continuation of negative feelings at the expense of team unity.

Great attention must be given to the selection of personnel. Coaches tend to look purely for talent down to the last player on the squad. In the first place this is unrealistic, because it is impossible to play everyone, and secondly, it does not provide for the establishment of team cohesion. When a talented player does not play, he is made to feel as though he is left out, ignored, or rejected. This may result in anger and come out in rebelliousness. Cliques, more often than not, start with the reserves who are unhappy, because their needs are not being met. The coach should strive to develop a strong team unity, rather than simply to gather "talent," by selecting those individuals who have the personal characteristics which lead to a strong team cohesiveness—loyalty, coachability, and perseverance. This is not to say that a coach should ignore talent. It is, of course, tremendously important, but as much consideration must be given to the individual's psychological characteristics.

The earlier a problem is faced, the higher the probability that a solution will be reached. If a problem is ignored, or if the coach feels it will simply "take care of itself," the more complex the problem may become. If problems persist to an unhealthy degree, the coach should seek professional advice.

chapter 7
MOTIVATION

Possibly the most important role played by the coach is that of motivator. His personality, convictions, goals, and motivational techniques are of primary importance to the development of the attitudes of his athletes and to the degree of success they will achieve. Therefore, he needs to inspect his own theory of motivation and to examine his views of those qualities he thinks are important in developing a winner. These same motivational concepts will very likely become a dominant part of his team's character, simply because these are the things he will emphasize most strongly. For example, if the dominant focus of attention by the coach is on organization, most likely his team will be a group of well-disciplined and organized athletes who know exactly what they are going to do. A coach who places a major emphasis on hard work will probably produce a team that is in superior physical condition and a team that also will appreciate the value of this conditioning. By the same token, undesirable personality traits will be passed on to the players and, in turn, become associated with their team. This general principle should seem reasonable to most coaches who constantly witness coaching philosophies toward styles of play produce teams that conform to those philosophies. For example, a great defensive coach produces great defensive teams; a manager who strongly believes in the value of the bunt has a team that becomes adept at this part of the game; and a coach who has become convinced that pressuring the opponent is necessary to win will produce teams that are known for this characteristic.

As a result of extra emphasis in one area, it is possible that a team will be deficient in another area. For example, a football coach may emphasize hitting so much that he forgets to teach his players to analyze a situation and handle it intelligently; an organized team may be so concerned with the form and mechanics of the game that they forget the importance of hitting. In other words, the coach *may* be sacrificing other important elements of play to stress his special area. For the "complete" approach to motivation, the following factors are critical:

1. The coach needs to examine his own philosophy about what is important (motivational factors).
2. He needs to examine his methods of putting his philosophy into effect (how he brings out these traits in his teams).
3. If his approach is not successful, he must decide what is needed to improve the situation.
4. He must become aware of the advantages and disadvantages of his own philosophy.
5. The coach should be able to see where he is falling short of the "complete" approach in the motivational scene.
6. The coach must be aware of how motivation works on a team level and how it affects the individual athlete. He should be familiar with the special techniques useful with teams and individual players devoid of these desired traits.
7. The coach also should make every effort to determine whether he is unconsciously doing anything that might undermine his motivational goals. A coach, for example, might emphasize hard work, yet cut his practices too short; another may stress hitting but not tolerate anger, swearing, or fighting on his team; a third may stress

organization and strategic planning, but be himself a careless person. It is not uncommon for coaches to have unrealistic expectations. The coach may genuinely be concerned about his club's lack of aggression without ever realizing that he is not an aggressive person himself and, therefore, is indirectly responsible for the situation.

A fair question to ask at this point is "Can a coach be a completely effective motivator in *all* aspects of play? Can he inspire aggressiveness, hard work, organization, and team spirit to equally high degrees?" Success *is* possible, but only if the coach *very carefully* analyzes the situation, plans his course of action, and then strictly adheres to the plan.

VERBAL MOTIVATION

As was mentioned previously, there are several forms and styles of communication with varying degrees of effectiveness. In general, the most common types associated with motivation are: pep talks; team talks or discussions; talks with the individual athlete.

To some coaches these talks will not be much of a problem, because the coaches are able to verbalize eloquently. Very effective coaches have a flair for the dramatic, and they are able to capture and excite the team with their inspirational speeches. They often have a genuine ability to make their feelings known to their players. Sincere and enthusiastic involvement with the players toward common goals is the most effective form of motivation. The athletes *should* be free to build common emotions and empathize with each other and with the coach.

BEHAVIORAL MOTIVATION

Rituals Emphasis on routine and habit are desirable when discussing techniques of play, but the emphasis should be shifted when trying to motivate athletes to perform well. Variety gets players motivated. Therefore, the coach should utilize varied motivational techniques. Changes of technique must be made discretely so as not to call attention to them.

Coaches, in their attempt to build good, solid, and lasting habits, depend upon repetition to establish desired characteristics, but a lack of variety may be responsible for late-season slumps. To avoid upsetting his players, no coach would think of changing the style of play in the middle of the season, but from the standpoint of motivation, a variety of techniques is precisely what accounts for a continually high degree of involvement by the players. There is a kind of security when the players know what is going to happen (game plan, plays, preconceived methods of handling special situations, etc.), but a coach must avoid the same kind of comfort and security in his motivational approach, because it will not keep his players fired up. Static approaches do not inspire. The same pep talk at every half time would fail to inspire. Different types of encouragement bring about more inspired play.

Gimmicks   Gimmicks may be a combination of verbal and behavioral motivation, or they may be just behavioral. Gimmicks are different from rituals in that they may be used in a special situation on a one shot basis: placing in the locker room the uncomplimentary comments made by the opponent in a newspaper clipping; awards for special efforts or accomplishments; pictures; slogans; signs; or special goals for a particular game.

REASONS FOR PARTICIPATION

The coach must make an effort to understand the motivational forces that stimulate the individual's athletic participation. The direction and extent of the coach's future efforts may be determined if he is able to accurately assess the initial degree of motivation present in the athlete.

If the player is bright, hard-working, aggressive, and loyal, the coach does not have to make any adjustments or do anything special. It may be a serious mistake, however, to assume that all athletes participate purely for the love of the sport. There may be many other reasons for participation, and they may vary tremendously from one individual to another. The athlete may participate:

1. To gain recognition
2. To feel more adequate (to feel more masculine)
3. To satisfy a parental desire
4. To impress a girlfriend
5. To provide himself with an opportunity for getting rid of his feelings of anger

By no means is this intended to be a definitive list. Rather, it merely suggests the existence of some reasons for playing other than pure love of the sport. The ultimate question here is would the player still continue to play with the same degree of enthusiasm if these motivating forces were removed, or if the opportunity for their realization was modified in some way? For instance, if the girlfriend or the parents were unable to come to the game, would the player's performance be affected? Would an increasing parental anxiety over potential college scholarships seriously alter the player's effectiveness? It is, of course, quite possible that the coach would have no control over some of these variables, but he should be aware of their existence so that he may help to avoid an unpleasant or discomforting situation if possible.

A serious philosophical disagreement may exist among coaches about the justification for athletic motivation. Some coaches feel that they should not have to motivate. They see athletic participation as a natural desire, and the attempt on the part of the coach to motivate as being out of place and unnecessary. Other coaches believe it is their responsibility to motivate the athlete. In the final analysis, the role of the coach as a motivator is inescapable, if he assumes it is his role to help each athlete realize his maximum potential.

How can a coach discover the true basis for his player's motivation? The player profile sheet in Chapter 5 will serve to provide the coach with some insight into this subject. Another approach is to ask the athlete directly, provided the coach feels the athlete is frank and honest enough to give the full story. Some athletes may find it necessary to tell the coach what they think he wants to hear in order to play, because the truth may be too threatening. A great many coaches might be surprised to find out the more personal reasons for their team members' participation in athletics.

MOTIVATIONAL PREPARATION

Careful motivational planning must take place before the season begins to insure against mishandling individual personalities and important situations affecting the entire team.

As for individual personalities, it is recommended that the coach make reference to the player profile sheet in Chapter 5 to guide him in the development of an individual motivation chart, which grows out of the information about the individual as described in Chapter 3.

By utilizing the information derived from the player profile sheet and by evaluating the effectiveness of various motivational techniques with different personality types, a guide for handling the individual can be easily established. If, for example, a particular player is highly motivated by having attention focused on him, the coach might consider the situation and, if desirable, arrange for this focusing of attention. The coach might arrange for a player with a great sense of pride to receive letters from alumni and former great players, or to be given a special uniform, number, or locker, or to be placed in a special position of leadership. The list of possible motivational needs and ways to answer them is enormous. Proper insight and careful consideration will dictate the proper course of action. Once the players' personalities are correctly analyzed and plans for individual motivation carefully developed, the expenditure of time required to carry them out will be minimal when compared with the benefits to be derived.

Motivation on a team level is equally important. Many situations will arise during the season to which the coach must respond intelligently and with perception. He may wish to go to the extent of outlining methods for handling his group in several conceivable situations such as:

1. Preparing to meet the traditional rival
2. Preparing to meet the expected league champion
3. Preparing for what the coach expects to be a big loss
4. Preparing for what appears to be an easy opponent
5. Recovering from the "slump"—that period in the season when nothing seems to be going right
6. Recovering from a close loss
7. Recovering from a severe loss
8. Directing the team after a close win
9. Directing the team after a big win
10. Preparing to meet a team that you have already beaten (by a close margin or by a large margin)
11. Preparing to meet a team to which you have already lost (by a close margin or by a large margin)
12. Creating interest in, and enthusiasm for, the practice session

Of course, a great deal depends upon the type of team with which the coach is working. Teams react differently to various situations based on their dominant personality traits. They can be tough, tender, aggressive, passive, ambitious, or lazy in the same way as individual players. The coach will have to adjust his handling to suit the team's special needs. Generally, though, he can begin by assuming that certain situations produce somewhat typical reactions in athletes, and by anticipating these reactions, he can help to alleviate some of the anxiety that will result. Table 3 illustrates some motivational techniques for handling different situations.

Table 3 is only a partial listing of situations requiring motivational handling. The examples given cover "typical"

TABLE 3. Motivating the Team for Competition

Situation	Handling
Preparing to meet the traditional rival	Remind the players in every possible way that they have a responsibility to others to carry on a tradition. Something has been handed down to them in trust, and it is their obligation to do their best to live up to valued traditions.
Preparing to meet the expected league champion	Make it clear that they are facing one of the biggest challenges they will have during the season. The team should point to the game as the prime test of their ability. Try to make it apparent to the players that this is what competition is all about. The fun of challenging the best is what provides the greatest thrills in athletics. Try to create an atmosphere of enthusiastic anticipation.
Preparing for what the coach expects to be a big loss	Avoid talk about winning and losing. Subtly make it clear to the players that end-results are not the most important thing. Set goals for individuals and work toward achieving as many of these as possible. Expect each person to do his very best.
Preparing for what appears to be an easy opponent	Stress that each individual must assume his own responsibility. Each person must be warned against easing up. Get personal commitments and realistically discuss what could happen.
Recovering from the "slump" —that period in the season when nothing seems to be going right	Ask *each individual* athlete to do his very best. Make it clear to him that the team is the coach's responsibility. Try to convince the athlete that his only concern should be himself and doing his own job to the very best of his ability.
Recovering from a close loss	Show concern for the disappointment felt by the athletes and the resultant letdown that follows. It may help a little to point out to them that close losses are most often due to breaks, and breaks even out during the season. By all means support them and express faith in them.

122

Recovering from a severe loss	The chief danger here is that the athletes may begin to feel inadequate and lose their desire and enthusiasm. To build confidence in the players, point out where they can improve and where they did well in the game. This is the time many coaches begin to punish their players or grow detached. There is nothing to be gained from this attitude except a further loss of confidence and resentment.
Directing the team after a close win	In this case, keep the momentum going. It will help to convince the players that they are "on their way." Point out areas for further improvement.
Directing the team after a big win	Same as handling them when preparing for an easy opponent. There is danger of complacency here. It would help to emphasize continuation of momentum.
Preparing to meet a team which you have already beaten (by a close margin or by a large margin)	Emphasize the superiority they have already established and point to the areas in which they were very successful in the last game. Play upon the confidence the athletes have gained from the first victory. Be *very* careful to guard against complacency.
Preparing to meet a team to which you have already lost (by a close margin or by a large margin)	Carefully see to it that the players do not become too disappointed and begin to develop a feeling of inadequacy against that opponent. It will help to point out specifically where they were beaten by the opponent in the first game and then set up goals for each individual to work toward. It might help to tell the players that this is the situation in which most upsets occur. Convince them they can win if they can accomplish specific goals.
Creating interest in, and enthusiasm for, the practice session	Above all else, employ variety in motivational techniques. The practices must be interesting, challenging, and enjoyable. The practices should be game-like and create a strong carry-over.

123

teams. The coach will want to vary his approach in accordance with his team's dominant personality traits to meet the *special* needs of his players.

The coach might keep his own personal log, recording what has been effective with different teams, to help guide him in his future efforts. That is, in each situation he would describe in detail the reactions of his players to his handling techniques. This would provide him with some kind of a guideline for handling similar problems when they arise in the future. By the same token, he would avoid techniques that failed.

In formulating his plans for motivational preparation, the coach should employ a dynamic approach to maintain variety and keep the players enthusiastically involved. The motivational planning will depend to a great extent on the schedule. It is virtually impossible to maintain maximum motivation for an extended period of time. This should be considered and provisions made not only for helping players through the psychologically difficult period, but also to help them reach periods of peak performance during the critical stages of the season.

There also will be periods during which almost nothing is required of the coach, because the players will have enough going for them already. When this happens, the coach should guard against motivating because he feels it is *expected* of him. He should also guard against motivating on the basis of his own personal anxiety. Some coaches motivate simply because they feel this is a "part" of their job, and their job is not complete unless they give the pep talk or employ a variety of gimmicks. At times the best motivation may be to say nothing.

The most successful form of motivation comes from the players themselves. If players are participating for their own reasons, their level of involvement will be considerably greater than if they are doing it for the coach. Some coaches, for example, "overhear" comments made by players during the game or on the way to the dressing room at half time and use this information as a source for building a pep talk. Some teams may be very angry at their inefficiency during the game and, in fact, want the coach to chew them out because they are doing so poorly. In these cases, it may be the very thing the team needs to spur them on. If the motivation grows out of the team's needs, it will be more effective.

MOTIVATIONAL TIMING

Essentially, motivational timing involves not only what to say, but also when to say it. It is assumed that the coach has prepared the athlete and outlined goals sufficiently for the motivational techniques to have some meaning and relevance for the individual. A few well chosen words at an appropriate time will be far more effective than a lengthy pep talk when the team is not listening or is not ready. It is often the coach's perception that determines how accurate his timing is. He may have nothing more than an intense feeling that a certain statement, behavior, or gimmick will motivate the team. In these instances, he must have faith in, and be willing to follow through with, such feelings. In time, he may be able to recognize more clearly what created such feelings.

Before the player can be effectively and significantly motivated he must:

1. Feel unique or special in some way
2. Be handled on a personal level
3. Clearly understand and agree with team goals

LONG-RANGE PREPARATION

When compared with game preparation, the motivational approach for seasonal goals is more general and flexible in its adherence to a plan of action. Goals may be altered as the coach observes a change in the characteristics and needs of the team. The initial planning must be somewhat loose because the coach cannot anticipate everything.

Seasonal goals must be established early. Directions and guidelines should be stressed along with a realistic assessment of the team's strengths. This should be followed by team discussions to give the players a voice in the establishment of policy. Essentially, the coach and the players concurrently provide answers to the question, "Where are we going?" With the answers to this question, the coach can begin to adjust his thinking about all aspects of play. Motivational preparation for an opponent should start much earlier than game preparation.

SHORT-RANGE PREPARATION

Short-range motivational preparation begins for the next game and opponent immediately after a contest is completed. The coach's approach has much to do with the results of the game. After a good game, the coach must make the effort to keep the players high; after a poor game, he must begin immediately to build their confidence. A loss requires a more concerted effort on the part of the coach, because he has to support the players and rebuild what has been lost.

To achieve a high degree of motivation, the coach should be prepared to alter the handling of each individual athlete after each contest. At one time, the player might be motivated on the basis of what he has just accomplished in the previous game. At another time, the coach may motivate by referring to the athlete's reason for playing. He might use background information about the athlete's parents, his girlfriend, his love of the sport, or the crowd. On another occasion the coach may emphasize the athlete's dominant personality traits—his intelligence, aggression, ambition. By altering these three motivational approaches (performance in the previous game, background data and reason for playing, and individual personality traits), the coach can maintain a high degree of enthusiastic involvement among his athletes.

PEP TALK

A large number of coaches and fans look upon the pep talk before the game or at half time as the coach's most important task. Many consider the pep talk as the full extent of the "psychological" approach. Tradition dictates its use and style, and many would not think of altering the custom.

Often an outsider (friend, fan, teacher, other coach) watching and listening to a coach at half time, uses the coach's performance as a measure of his greatness. In response, some coaches react as though it is curtain time— they are "on" and they know it. They tend to use, sometimes without thought, what they feel has been successful for them in the past. If a survey of coaches were made to determine the meaning of coaching psychology, very probably the majority would list the pep talk as the most important example of its use with athletes. Because of this feeling, therefore, the pep talk must be considered an important part of the coaching world.

Why the pep talk? It is given with a specific purpose in mind and, although it may appear spontaneous, it is usually planned. The purpose most often is to inspire the athlete to do better.

The pep talk is directly associated with the actual competitive situation. It is so closely related to the act of competition timewise that it really cannot be separated from the act itself. It is given to some degree in an emotional way because that is what inspires the players. An athletic contest is an emotional experience. It is more than a situation requiring strategy in a detached manner. The coach wants to get the player to go out on the field as emotionally high as when he is competing. He cannot play in the locker room, of course, but the emotions can be aroused to the point they will reach during the contest. If the players are not "ready" and have to build momentum during the game itself, or overcome an unexpected high level of attack, they may be beaten before they really have a chance. The coach needs to inspire, but he also needs to have players control their emotions. Otherwise, they might become so excited that they would be ineffective. Pep talks are more likely to inspire younger and more immature players.

The pep talk may assume many different forms. At times, it may deal with a specific team trait; at other times, with a specific team attitude. A beginning of the game pep talk is usually a more general thing, inspiring in the athletes the desire to go out and perform at a high level from the beginning of the contest. In the pre-game pep talk, the coach does not necessarily have to focus on a specific area of play. The half time pep talk deals with more specific things, because an adjustment is necessary. For example, a team may be told they are getting hurt off-tackle, on the boards, or because of a lack of aggression, and quick adjustments are outlined. If a team has been successful in the first half, the coach may simply reinforce and reemphasize the importance of maintaining the advantage. Whether the talk should be long or short depends upon the nature of the team and the events that have taken place in the contest.

Regardless of the approach taken or the amount of time spent, immediately before the players leave the dressing room the coach will want to emphasize what he considers to be the most important piece of information.

Assuming there are no particularly difficult team problems, the methods outlined in Table 4 may help guide the coach at half time. A variety of circumstances are described along with the expected player reactions and the recommended techniques for handling the problem.

The coach must realize that he also may possess, in varying degrees, the five qualities listed in Table 4. He must be in tune with how he feels about these characteristics, because it will influence how he will react at half time. If he has some objective assessment of how he and the team might feel in each of the situations, he will be better able to cope with the difficulty. The coach can objectively set up and carefully consider every conceivable possibility ahead of time, and, by so doing, be prepared to deal with the situation that arises.

INTERNAL MOTIVATION

The degree of internal motivation varies greatly among athletes. The reason for participation and the extent to which they are prepared to work to achieve success are factors with which the coach has very little to do—at least at first. Some athletes are highly motivated internally. They will spend an enormous amount of time working to perfect their skills without ever being prodded or cajoled by the coach. Others spend very litle time, and the coach must work to provide the motivation necessary to help them reach their potential. Most of the time it is fairly obvious who is motivated and to what degree. The athlete who stays after practice to work on his skills and the player who regularly showers first and leaves before the others are both easy to spot.

EXTERNAL MOTIVATION

A problem facing all coaches is motivating the athlete externally while, at the same time, providing him with information regarding his play. The coach can have the player do what he wants by both praising and punishing. The difference is that with praise the athlete will end up with a more positive attitude toward the coach, the competition, and himself.

Praise gives the athlete an idea of what is correct. Punishment does not. It tells him that he is wrong. It does nothing toward building positive feelings. Reward for proper execution of a skill builds the player's confidence and helps him achieve more success in the other areas of play. Punishment creates doubt and confusion in the player regarding his own ability and the coach's ability to help him. It is like giving a person the keys to a car, telling him where you want to go, but not telling him how to get there. He may have no idea at all of where he is or how to get where he is asked to go. At every wrong turn he hears, "You

TABLE 4. Motivating a Team at Half Time

Ahead at half time	Expected to win	Expected to lose
	High	*High*
	Maintain the challenge. There may be a let-down. The team must be kept high, desiring even more.	The players must be supported. They should be reassured of their ability to do it all along. The individual is probably at his peak of per-formance.
Desire	*Low*	*Low*
	There may be a tendency to let down. They must be encouraged to keep up the momen-tum they have going.	There is a fear of giving up here. They feel they have already proven themselves. The coach needs to emphasize that it is the whole game that counts.
	High	*High*
	They respond to most techniques.	They respond to most techniques.
Self-confidence	*Low*	*Low*
	Maintain a high feeling. Express a faith in the players.	Overcome fear of falling behind. Encourage the players and try to convince them that it is not a fluke. Reassure them that they really can do it.

Emotional Stability	*High* They respond to most techniques. *Low* The players may become overly emotional. The coach must become the control. Emphasize keeping cool. The players may react as though they had already won.	*High* They respond to most techniques. *Low* The players may get cocky or flaky. The coach also has to serve as a control.
Toughness	*High* They respond to most techniques. *Low* The coach must continue to support, build up, and reassure the athletes.	*High* They respond to most techniques. *Low* There is a fear of falling behind. The coach must see to it that the players maintain the pace and not change style or begin to worry.
Responsibility	*High* Should be no problem. *Low* Should be no problem.	*High* Should be no problem. *Low* Should be no problem.

TABLE 4. (Continued)

Behind at half time		Expected to win	Expected to lose
Desire	*High*	Place a challenge before them. The players will be excited. The coach needs to direct that force and to challenge them to prove their worth and come back.	Challenge the team to beat the overwhelming odds. The players will still be high. Can they face a really tough challenge?
	Low	The coach must overcome discouragement. He will have to pick up the players, reassure them, and emphasize their strong points.	The coach must overcome a sense of futility. One of the most difficult situations. Work on individuals primarily. Try to get individuals to spark the team. Work with individual motivations. Ignore trying to appeal to their spirit to combat the other team.
Self-confidence	*High*	They respond to most techniques.	They respond to most techniques.
	Low	Reduce anxiety. Overcome feelings of anxiety and inadequacy. Encourage and point out errors and ways of correcting them. Reassure the players that things will be all right when errors are corrected.	Fight feelings of futility. A good place to use gimmicks. Try to make the players feel worthwhile. Use any technique that will make the players feel more competent.

132

	Column 1	Column 2
Emotional Stability	*High* — They respond to most techniques.	*High* — They respond to most techniques.
	Low — This is where the players may begin to fall apart. Coach must clearly define expectations and regain control.	*Low* — The coach must clearly define areas of responsibility. He should avoid any kind of pep talk or emotional involvement.
Toughness	*High* — The players should receive a tough chewing out. This is the place for a fight talk.	*High* — Fight talk and chewing out is also appropriate here.
	Low — There will be a fear of punishment or of doing badly. Chewing them out would cause a problem.	*Low* — Tough but supportive. Encourage the players to do the very best they possibly can.
Responsibility	*High* — The coach must relieve the guilt. Point out actual reasons for failure and clarify assignments.	*High* — Follow the same basic plan.
	Low — Avoid blaming anyone. Deal with individuals.	*Low* — Players will blame others. Coach must define responsibility.

133

stupid idiot, that's not the way to go!" He is never told clearly in what direction to go; he is only told that he is going in the wrong direction.

For effective verbal motivation, the following steps are suggested:

1. *Open with praise.* The coach should mention an area of play which in his *honest* opinion, has been strong for the player. This supports the athlete and makes him feel capable by pointing out an area in which he is succeeding.
2. *Make the correction or suggestion.* The coach should report objective, factual material to the athlete about what he is doing and how it may be done more effectively.
3. *End by complimenting.* Finally, the coach should tell the player that with a little practice, he will be fully capable of improving the weak areas of his play, because he *is* a good and competent athlete.

A coach talking to the athlete and using the three steps discussed might sound like this: "Bob, you're doing a great job with your handoffs. It sure makes a difference in the way our offense goes. That extra effort you've been putting in is sure paying off." (Next comes the correction.) "You might give some more time to your drop back time and release of the ball. It could be a little faster and it would allow you to get off the pass without rushing it." (At this point, the athlete may be unhappy with himself for not picking up the skill properly, but this feeling can be taken care of with another word from the coach.) "But that shouldn't be too much of a problem for you. You'll pick it up just as well as you did the handoffs. The effort and time you're spending is great! Keep it up."

The compliment opened him up; he let down his guard, and the information was presented. Then, he was left with praise. This particular approach is most effective with very sensitive athletes who find it very difficult to accept any suggestions from the coach.

There *are* times when a coach can get legitimately angry and handle a player very roughly. This may be the case when a player consistently breaks a rule; or if he is harming himself, the team, or his fellow players through a lack of effort. In this case, anger is a show of concern.

To get angry at a player because he is not intelligent, because he does not understand, because he is confused, or because he is frightened usually has a detrimental effect on the athlete's performance. It only succeeds in relieving the coach's anger. It has nothing to do with helping the athlete.

The time when a coach is most likely to get angry is when he has instructed the athlete, and the athlete still does not perform the skill correctly. The coach becomes mad and directs his anger at the person rather than at the inability to execute the skill. To the athlete, the coach's general tone suggests, "You dumb clod, you're worthless!"

Getting angry not only does not help, but also makes the situation worse. Of course, this is assuming that the athlete is genuinely trying. If he is genuinely trying and is still not picking up the skill successfully, the coach's anger at that particular moment will work against their mutual benefit.

If the player is not picking up the information because he is not paying attention or because he is lazy, then he needs to be attacked on that basis. This is a legitimate reason for the coach's anger, because the athlete is not only breaking a rule, but also harming himself.

There are several reasons why a player does not pick up some information successfully and make satisfactory improvement:

1. He may not be intelligent enough. To get angry at the player because he is not smart enough is not going to help him pick up the skill and improve. It will have no effect whatsoever on his I.Q. For this person, the coach needs to make the instructions very simple, and he must be certain that the athlete understands exactly what is expected of him.

2. He may not thoroughly comprehend all of the implications of what the coach is talking about. He may be bright enough, but there is, for some reason, something interfering with communication. Possibly the coach is not making completely clear to the athlete what he ex-

pects. Getting angry at the person because the coach has not made an approach clear is not good. Quite often anger is an attempt by the coach to absolve himself of the blame for the player's poor performance. It would be best to ask the player to repeat the instructions to determine his level of understanding.

3. He may be disturbed to the point that he is unable to think or receive information intelligently, because he knows he has made an error, or because he is failing to execute the skill properly. His emotion begins to interfere with his thinking and actions. To get angry with him because he is scared or emotional is only going to make him more emotional and interfere with effective communication. In this case, the coach should not even deal with the information. He should support the player by talking to him, calming him down, and helping him overcome the emotional crisis which is interfering with the communication.

In terms of instruction, the coach must avoid becoming angry at the person. He certainly will be angry often at the way a technique is being executed, but there is never any reason to get angry at someone when instructing him. Ordinarily, those who provoke the feeling of anger are the ones who need the greatest support, understanding, strength, and time.

A coach may have the ability to look at the player and determine the reason for the lack of communication. He may be able to discover the cause for the trouble by watching very carefully to see how the player is reacting (dilation of eyes, shaking, nervous actions, blank look, not paying attention, etc.) and avoid a conflict before it arises.

Again, if a player is not picking up a skill because he does not care or because he is not listening, the coach has every right to attack the motivation (or lack of it). "Look, if you don't want to play ball, just tell me. If you want to play ball, you're going to have to listen and put in the time!"

Sometimes the coach will sound as though he is punishing the player when he is chewing him out, but, in truth, he is building the athlete's confidence, because his anger is expressed in a positive manner. For example, the coach might say, "I'm sick and tired of you being beaten by that guy—you're bigger, and stronger, and better than he is, and he's really clobbering you. Now I want to see you go out there and get him!" An approach such as this can actually leave a player feeling superior and supported even though there is anger involved.

To summarize, instruction and punishment are very separate acts. The coach must instruct, but punishment need not enter the picture. It is a very poor substitute for instruction. As a matter of fact, it is the poorest form that could be devised.

There will be a few players with whom the coach will not be able to work, no matter how hard he tries. Before the coach finally gives up on the player completely, he might try a direct confrontation. He can be extremely open with the person by telling him exactly how he feels about him and by giving him an honest evaluation of his performance. There need be no anger involved, but the coach can make it clear to the athlete that his membership on the team is over unless he does certain very specific things within very specific time periods. If this approach fails, the coach can feel perfectly secure that he has done his best. He knows he has done everything possible to get the desired results from the player, and any further effort on his part would simply be a waste of time.

chapter 8
DISCIPLINE

All aspects of athletic participation (from the team member to the solitary competitor) require that the person adhere to some rather rigid guidelines. Discipline may be defined as the attempt to set limitations to modify behavior.

The wide variety of motivational needs and the great divergence in personality types within a team make it difficult to develop a standard approach to discipline. Some individuals have a highly developed ability to discipline themselves, while others possess very little self-control. Again the coach must adapt his handling techniques to the needs of the individual. His requirement is to assess those needs, set up the proper regimen, and maintain the type of discipline which, in his opinion, is necessary for success.

Discipline has many facets. The rules and regulations of the game itself require that certain restrictions be imposed on the athletes. For example, a player is allowed only three strikes in baseball, and if he goes offside in football he is penalized five yards. Of course it would be nice to have four or five strikes or to be able to get the quarterback before the ball was snapped, but chaos would result from non-adherence to these rules, which are enforced as uniformly as is humanly possible. So, discipline in athletics is often imposed on the participants by "outside" influences—referees, umpires, and judges. From the beginning of their competitive lives, most participants learn to accept the rules and disciplines of the game or the penalties that result when the rules are broken.

Athletics require discipline in three major areas. If a player lacks sufficient self-control in any of these areas, the coach must assume command of the situation. The three areas are:

1. Acquisition and maintenance of physical condition
2. Development of emotional control
3. Creation of proper image

The athlete must exercise great physical control in preparing for competition. Successful game plans and effective physical skills are the result of perseverance and attention to detail in a highly organized manner.

A high degree of emotional discipline is required during competition. The athlete learns early that he is expected not to cry or to get publicly angry. There is a kind of tacit understanding that players will not do certain things—they do not get too rough, they do not hurt people unnecessarily (without risking serious reprisal by the other team), and they do not show pain. These restraints and many more are accepted without discussion or question by the individual. These "weaknesses" do occur, certainly, but there is general disdain for the person guilty of committing them.

Some may be concerned about including the creation of proper image under discipline. Because the team comes before the public, the players and the coach have the responsibility to adhere to the rules of good conduct in an attempt to establish and maintain an image acceptable to the school or organization they represent. Part of the coach's responsibility here is to serve as a parental surrogate. He is also a representative of society, since he is responsible for his players' behavior, even outside the school environment. The coach is held accountable for his players' actions to a much greater extent than any other member of the faculty. It is not uncommon to hear a person refer to the individual's affiliation with a sport when speaking critically of his conduct, "Look at that basketball player smoking and drinking." It is ludicrous to imagine that same criticism being directed at any other group. The statement, "Look at that *history* student smoking and drinking," makes no sense, or has very little meaning.

DISCIPLINARY APPROACH

Each coach has his own philosophy of discipline. The degree and extent to which it is applied must be decided by the individual coach and must be in keeping with his personal philosophy of handling athletes. It should be mentioned, however, that certain advantages and disadvantages are inherent in the various types of philosophies.

A few coaches share the view that each player should be allowed the freedom to select and maintain his own schedule of activity. This approach requires the athlete to exhibit a great sense of self-direction, which is a lot to expect of any person, particularly a young athlete who undertakes such a program. Some athletes are quite capable of directing themselves, but most are in a poor position to objectively judge what is best for them without having very extensive knowledge of the sport. Obviously in some sports this would be less of a problem than in other sports.

In individual sports, for example, it is somewhat easier to develop and maintain an individual schedule than in team sports, simply because team sports require coordination and effort by several people. The other extreme is much more commonly practiced by coaches on all levels. They take almost complete and absolute control of the athlete in every possible way. They establish a great many rules and severely punish the athlete when the rules are broken. Perhaps this is best illustrated by professional football in which curfews are enforced by bed checks and fines, weight (to the pound) is dictated and again enforced through fines, and exact times for practices, arrivals, and departures are established. Necessity usually dictates most of these rules and, if they are considered fair by the team, they will be accepted and will help strengthen team cohesion.

Too many rules are difficult, if not impossible, to enforce. With everyone going through the same routines and rituals and following the same rules and regulations, it is easy to develop spirit, particularly if success is present. Rules that the team feels are unfair, irrelevant, or due to the coach's idiosyncrasies may cause resentment and may lead to an attempt by the team to break them.

The large majority of coaches are flexible enough to use several methods of discipline and are able to adjust the situation to fit the person. One of the characteristics most commonly attributed to a coach is his ability to handle men. He is seen by most as a tough disciplinarian. This image can become a problem for some coaches. In many instances, they find that other teachers in their school attempt to use the athletic situation and the coach as an avenue of approach to punish individuals for inadequate or inappropriate behavior in the classroom. For example, a teacher may ask the coach to handle what, for that teacher, is a difficult problem, "Tom is not doing well in class. He is very irregular about handing in his homework and is responsible for most of my discipline problems. If his behavior doesn't improve I'm going to have to speak to Mr. Molloy about having him dropped from after school sports." This displaced discipline routine is not at all unusual and most coaches have experienced it.

The request to help with a problem or to talk with the student-athlete about being more responsible is not unreasonable. It becomes unreasonable, however, when punishment is inflicted on the athlete for his unacceptable behavior or for his unsatisfactory effort as a student in the classroom. It is like having the coach come to the classroom teacher and say, "Tom didn't do well on the practice field today. Will you make sure he gets an extra assignment in English as punishment? I just can't handle him on the football field. He's thinking too much about English to really do a good job in football. He doesn't have his mind on the game. For example, the other day we were in the middle of this spirited scrimmage, and there he was over by the sidelines talking about Shakespeare! I'm afraid if his attitude doesn't improve I'll have to see about getting him removed from the classroom."

This is, of course, a facetious line of reasoning, but every coach knows it has its foundation in fact. Perhaps a more realistic way of handling the problem would be to say to the teacher, "Yes, I will be glad to tell Tom that you're not able to handle his behavior and that you're asking me to punish him for you." The coach's obligation may be such that he is required to take action, but at least it is an honest presentation of the facts and will not lead to an alienation of the athlete.

DEVELOPMENT OF A DISCIPLINARY CODE

It is extremely rare to have a winner who is not disciplined. The development of talent and the nature of both the practice and the game requires a high degree of control. Some aspects of discipline that the coach might keep in mind in developing his own disciplinary code are the following:

The rule should be relevant.   The rules established by the coach should be relevant to the activity and to the situation. In football, for example, reasonable training rules, proper food, and curfews dictated by the coach are relevant, because conditioning is an understandable part of success. If, however, the coach insists that everybody brush his teeth with Colgate every morning during the season, it is totally irrelevant to athletic success and may account for team unrest.

The rule should be fair.   There is a belief among some athletes today that they should be left relatively on their own to make decisions about what is best for them and should be free to determine for themselves the direction in which they will travel. In the individual sports—tennis, golf, swimming, track, etc.—this may be true to some degree, but in a team sport, it is totally untrue. In a team sport, discipline goes well beyond the individual effort, and each athlete must make the decision to either accept the discipline or leave the team. Since he cannot change the rules of the game, it is unreasonable for him to expect to change the rules of discipline—if they are fair. Rules and regulations are set down by coaches as a part of their professional responsibility. The players have a responsibility to abide by those rules as long as they remain members of the team. Ill-feeling may arise as a result of the individual's concern that he is being forced to compromise some aspect of his individuality to become a member of the team. The coach may be flexible enough to alter some of his team rules if he feels the athlete's requests are reasonable. If he feels they represent too much of a selfish attitude on the part of the player, he should simply say, "I can respect your feelings and your wanting to maintain your individuality, but I have a professional responsibility to decide what is best for our team. This includes asking the players to sacrifice some things that are important to them. In my opinion, the present rules must hold. If you're not willing to accept them, I can accept your resignation from the squad. The decision is yours to make."

It is important to make the distinction between the establishment of discipline and authoritarianism. When the coach is aware of the individual needs of each athlete, along with the uniqueness of his team (and makes adjustments accordingly when establishing and maintaining rules of discipline), he is not authoritarian. The athletes are more important than the rules. The coach who demands blind obedience, regardless of the individual needs of the athlete, is authoritarian. The athletes feel less important, and many may be made to suffer needlessly. In the first instance the coach acts as if human beings made the rules; in the second instance, the coach acts as if human beings were slaves to the rules.

Before making rules regarding the athletes' personal habits, the coach should consider four things: team image; effectiveness of performance; personal attitudes toward the team; and the individual feelings of the players. If the athletes' personal habits negatively affect any of the above, rules must be imposed.

Perhaps the most difficult responsibility to explain or to justify to others deals with the player's attitude toward personal sacrifice for the good of the team. A player's willingness to lose some of his own identity for the good of the team is the intangible foundation of great team spirit. Adherence to a rule may be symbolic of the degree of personal sacrifice the player is willing to make. Generally, if the player gets upset with having to conform to relatively minor rules, the coach will likely have some problems with the player in other areas.

The coach must exercise good judgment in the area of discipline. For example, if he has a personal prejudice and this prejudice is the sole reason for the rule, then the rule is not justified. Adherence to this type of rule forces the athlete to totally subjugate his personal self to the prejudicial will of the coach. This disciplinary approach is not good for it represents a kind of fanaticism by the coach requiring the athlete's absolute submission.

The feelings of the individual player deserve attention, but to expect a coach to immediately change a strong conviction about important issues is unrealistic. It is a rare thing for a person to admit that his thinking may not have been completely fair, but the players deserve and are entitled to an intelligent answer when they ask the question, "Why?" Most ask little more. The important thing is that the coach gives reasonable and fair answers.

The athlete who comes to the coach and says, "I want to be on the team, but your rules and regulations are infringing on my individual rights," has a rather one-sided opinion as to the nature of athletic participation. The coach is entitled to his philosophy as well. He can say, "You have the right to decide whether you want to be a member of this team. I have my rights and responsibilities as the coach to decide what is best for the team. I think these rules and regulations are necessary. I'm not taking away your rights —you are free to accept them or not. It is my professional judgment that these rules will help us become a successful team. I base my judgments on my knowledge, as well as on my training and experience. The rules of the team are as important as the strategy. They are part of my philosophy."

The coach, as a professional educator, must decide the image he wants for his team. This puts him in the position of the decision-maker, but the decision must be just. The coach must decide how much sacrifice his athletes must make to achieve the image, just as he must decide when the team will practice, how long, and where. To some athletes, this may seem like a dictatorship, to others, professional responsibility.

The rule should hold for everybody. The coach cannot make exceptions—at least not to the degree where he shows favoritism. Some legitimate exceptions will have to be made, but never to benefit one player at another's expense. For example, a player may miss bed check because of an illness in his family. To punish the person in this case would be totally unfair and would alienate him completely. To expect an injured player to run the required laps like everyone else is unreasonable, but to permit an individual to violate these rules without justification is equally poor procedure.

The team should be completely aware of what will happen if the rule is broken. To impose a penalty that had not been discussed beforehand with the team can create strong feelings of animosity toward the coach. For example, it would be an extremely bad policy to suspend a player for leaving on a trip without a coat and tie if he had never been informed of the rules regarding dress and the penalties to be inflicted on the violators.

The team should feel they are part of the rule-making body. Rules will be much more effective if the players have taken part in their creation. They should be somewhat democratic, or at least not totally determined by the idiosyncracies of the coach. A discussion of the rules with the team will help the coach to determine whether the players feel they are fair. The athletes' personal commitments to the rules may occur spontaneously. If this happens, a big part of the coach's problem is solved. Some team rules should be set by the coach alone, because they are relevant to his philosophy. Other rules, such as severity of punishment, the team may determine for themselves. In most cases the rules will be fair, and the players will be much more willing to abide by them.

For the penalty to be effective, it should be imposed immediately. At the time the violation is detected, the coach should impose the penalty. To punish a player for something he did two weeks ago is ineffective, because he will feel he is being punished for something that did not exist. For example, a coach learns that a player has broken a rule, but does nothing about it at the time. A week later during a scrimmage the coach, unhappy with the athlete's performance, makes reference to the week-old violation and punishes him for it at that moment. This is unfair and ineffective. To be effective, the penalty must be imposed immediately.

The penalties imposed should be commensurate to the crime. Nothing alienates a player faster than penalties which are too severe. A democratic, fair, and relevant rules system, which imposes only clear cut penalties that are commensurate to the infraction, will set controls for the coach and give him some peace of mind. After the system is established, there is never any reason to become emotionally upset if the rules are broken. The coach disciplines in accordance with the guidelines agreed upon by the group. Some coaches make the serious mistake of using the rule infraction as an excuse to punish an athlete. Punishment must not be a personal thing. It should relate to the act and not to the person.

The question coaches most often ask about discipline is how to get the respect of the players. Nothing gains the respect of the athlete more than intelligent organization. It is the most basic tool of discipline. A coach who knows what he is talking about and demonstrates it with his every action in a precise, detailed, and systematic way will inspire an extremely high degree of confidence in his athletes.

One of the goals of all athletic programs should be to help produce men who are willing and able to accept discipline. As was stated earlier in the book, participation in athletics represents a scaled-down version of life, and it is expected that a player will accept certain requirements in the competitive situation as he would in life. It is to be hoped also that the external disciplines of a team will become an integral part of the development of the person.

chapter **9**
TEACHING TECHNIQUES IN ATHLETICS

Coaches are teachers, and as teachers they are, or should be, familiar with the principles involved in the process of learning. A teacher or a coach unfamiliar with the principles of learning may have to rely on trial and error procedures and dictatorial methods of instruction to reach the desired goals. To avoid this, the coach should evaluate his methods of instruction to determine their degree of effectiveness in accomplishing his objectives. There is no consistent agreement among educators as to the best methods of instruction, but a few ideas are presented here for the coach's consideration.

ADJUSTING TO THE ATHLETE'S SKILLS

Learning curve   The learning curve depends upon the subject being learned and the person doing the learning, but there are certain trends that occur during the process which can be anticipated. At the beginning of the period of instruction, the coach will most likely find that the initial degree of success is great. This is due primarily to the high level of interest on the part of the participants in the new

activity. This is usually followed by a leveling off period
during which time the coach may feel that little or no progress is being made. This will cause some coaches to be discouraged and even to consider changing to other techniques
or styles of play as a substitute for what appears to be
failure. However, the athletes are only going through a
process of establishment and refinement of skills, making it
appear that the learning process has stopped. Most teams
experience this plateau, but some experience it for longer
periods than others. The important thing the coach must
keep in mind is this: if the style of play is sound and the
method of teaching has been effective, there is no need for
panic; the "crisis" will pass, and the cumulative effect of
the instruction will result in a sharp rise in team effectiveness near the end of the season.

Intelligence level   The coach must have accurate ways of
determining the degree of brightness of his athletes. He
must also realize that many will find it difficult to transfer
the information they have received mentally to the motor
level. It might help for the coach to obtain the I.Q. scores
of his players so that he will know at what level to aim his
instruction initially. The learning ability of the group will
determine two things: the speed with which he presents
material; and the degree of complexity of the material presented. Individual differences in the athletes must be recognized and adjustments made where necessary. The coach
is making a serious mistake if he expects all players to learn
at the same rate, or if he insists that all players use exactly
the same form in performing the skills.

It may help to give periodic quizzes to determine how
much the athletes are picking up. Many athletes will do well
in the traditional intelligence tests, but, in the periodic
quizzes given by the coach, the same athletes may not show
what most coaches call "athletic sense"—the ability to perform instinctively to a high degree of effectiveness. Con-
versely, some players will excel in the competitive situation
and be sadly lacking in intelligence test scores. The coach,
however, should expect a high degree of overlapping in the

two areas—that is, the person who scores well on intelligence tests is likely to grasp athletic fundamentals quickly.

Motivational level   Before really effective learning can take place, the player's interest and desire must be stimulated to the point where he is not only more receptive to instruction, but also actually desirous of it. If the player wants to succeed and is led to believe that the coach is in a position to help him obtain his goals, his powers of concentration will increase significantly. In the instances where the athlete feels compelled to practice, the interest level will be low and his performance will suffer. We are really dealing with the player's motivational level, but there are other factors to be considered. The person must feel that the goals are obtainable and that he is capable of handling the coach's instructions. Therefore, the complexity of instruction, the level of competition, and the degree of individual maturation and aspiration must be harmonious. To achieve success, these factors must not be in conflict with each other. If the athlete feels the goals are unobtainable, he will feel it is futile to attempt them and will give up. The coach should know each player's capacity and not go beyond it.

It is very important that the coach select stimulating activities to motivate the players to learn and practice. To do this, the coach should become familiar with the physical, mental, and emotional characteristics of the players with whom he will be dealing.

How can a coach know who is paying attention, and how can he handle players if they are not? Spot questions can help insure that everybody stays alert. In the middle of an explanation or demonstration, the coach should turn to an athlete and ask him to demonstrate his assignment. This method will become a part of his teaching technique. The coach must make it clear beforehand that he will ask questions of the players for the purpose of knowing which of them is paying attention.

When a player does not know the answer to a question, instead of getting angry and ridiculing him, the coach should direct the same question to someone else. To avoid unnecessary embarrassment, it is advisable that the next person asked be someone who plays the same position as the person who was unable to answer the question. It does no good to make a fool of the player for not knowing. He may have had a lapse in memory, or he may not have understood the instruction.

To develop more cohesiveness and to avoid having the players feel they are being picked on, early in the season the coach should pick out the players on the team who can demonstrate or answer the questions. This will instill confidence in the others. Never search for players who you think might not be listening to answer questions just to humiliate them. Nothing will alienate a player faster than being ridiculed in the learning situation. Make a point of rotating so that each player gets the opportunity to demonstrate or answer correctly. In this way all will become a part of the learning process.

The coach should not pick on the slow learner, especially during the first part of the season. Other players not only will lose confidence in that athlete, but also will begin to dislike the coach. Fear can spread. After a period of time has elapsed, the coach may direct questions at the slow learner, but he should use a simple situation to increase the player's confidence. If the player cannot answer the question, he still should be supported by the coach.

The coach can set up a good learning situation by saying, "I challenge anyone here in this room to show us how they can defeat this tactic." Often athletes want to rebel against authority figures, and a positive form of mental exercise such as this will give the players that opportunity. This gets the players actively involved in thinking about the play. The comments must be saved for a special time during the meeting, otherwise some individuals would be interrupting the coach's instruction and challenging him all the time.

If a question does come up, it is a good technique to turn it back to the group by saying, "Now can anyone answer that?" This starts discussion and thought. Players can both question the approach and defend it at the same time. The coach must never use this technique when he does not know the answer. He will lose the respect of the players. It is much better to say, "I don't know the answer to that question. Does anybody here know?" However, the coach may offer an opinion or tell the team he will make a point of finding the answer and will explain it later.

The coach may wish to give non-playing grades for effort that are separate from the actual performance. In this way, a knowledgeable player who is deficient in talent still can feel an important part of the team. It will give him a chance to receive recognition for his excellence. An award might even be given to a player at the end of the season for his outstanding knowledge and understanding of the game. This may be a person to whom the coach has turned for advice during the season. For his knowledge and insight, the player will feel respected.

A technique some coaches may find valuable is to have certain individuals on the team study specific areas of team play. It would be their duty to become extremely well-informed in their assigned area (man-to-man defense, zone offense, breaking the press). They may then help with instruction, be consulted by the coach when there is difficulty in that area, or submit reports evaluating the team's performance in that area during games or practices.

If a team can reach a point where the athletes do some of the teaching, it will improve team communication, cohesion, and motivation. It is one thing to have respect for authority, but it is another thing to become totally dependent upon the coach. A team that has to wait for everything to come from the coach will be lost in some situations.

TEACHING THE SKILLS

Clear and precise instruction   The first time the coach attempts to teach a technique, he should go through it very, very slowly. If possible, he should explain and demonstrate step-by-step and provide reasons for each of the steps. He must take special pains to see to it that the technique is done correctly the first few times. If it is learned incorrectly or unsatisfactorily, the player not only will have to learn something new in the future, but also may have to unlearn something that was a part of his past instruction.

A common problem is faced by coaches when they take over a position from someone else. The system or techniques the coach teaches may be confusing or in conflict with what was taught by the former coach. A coach taking a new position might find it profitable to inquire about the previous system in order to determine where his ideas and techniques overlap with those used previously. The same is true for totally new areas. The coach's biggest concern will be trying to teach a system that may be in conflict with the old system. If the old system has been learned very well, the athletes will tend to revert to the old system when they are under stress. In order to overcome this, the coach must spend extra time and effort with the team. In fact, the team should *overlearn* the new system. (Overlearning is discussed fully later in the chapter.)

The coach should try to minimize the complexities of the game and place everything in an orderly and logical sequence. The less confusion the better.

The language of instruction should be simple and consistent. The coach often falsely assumes that the players understand the terminology and the basics of play. Proper labeling of plays and techniques is important. The labels given them should be accurate and not in conflict with other aspects of play.

Most importantly, the material should be as well organized as the coach can make it. He must know that the athletes clearly understand what is expected of them in terms of timing, positioning, execution, and responsibilities. The only way to achieve this is through careful and consistent organization.

The coach must not assume that the athlete understands the instruction, because he does not ask questions. It will help for the coach to make sure he has the players' attention by maintaining eye contact with them. If he thinks an athlete does not understand he might ask him to repeat the instruction or, better yet, teach the skill to another player in the same position. A very successful means of involving all the players completely is to have them take turns teaching or coaching their teammates. If they are told ahead of time that this will occur, it will serve as an excellent means of motivation.

Proper demonstration There is, for many, a big gap between what is on the blackboard and what is to take place on the field of play. Seeing X's and O's on the board is one thing and involves one kind of learning; performing it on the field is another thing and involves another type of learning. The first involves a mental response, and the second involves a motor response. What may be perfectly understandable in the classroom may become totally confusing on the field. Certain kinds of people cannot tie the two together. These people must be taught only on the field of play.

The demonstration should be as nearly perfect as possible, because the players are really being asked to imitate. The coach will want to take advantage of every opportunity possible to have his players see highly skilled competitors performing in their sport. A great deal can be gained by watching others, not only from a technical standpoint, but also as a means of stimulating the younger players to become more enthusiastically involved in their commitment to the sport. The model selected should represent what the coach wishes to convey in his instruction. Motion pictures, photographs, illustrations, and drawings can serve to make clear to the athlete what the coach expects. The player must be encouraged to ask questions, which will help him understand how to properly execute the skill.

Accurate execution Accuracy and speed certainly go together in successful athletic performance, but the coach's initial emphasis should be placed on accuracy in the execution of an athletic skill. The old adage "learn to walk before running" is applicable in athletic instruction.

Positive reinforcement A player tends to learn quickly and repeat those reactions which are accompanied or immediately followed by something that brings satisfaction;

he tends not to repeat or learn rapidly those reactions which are accompanied or immediately followed by something that is annoying. Disapproval and criticism by the coach will be painful to the athlete and will help to increase his anxiety. If a player misses a tackle, it is already painful enough for him without the coach adding to his misery through criticism. The important thing the coach must remember is that criticism tends to destroy, rather than build, desirable traits in the person. It does little for him in the way of learning a skill. Reward and praise are much more effective in influencing behavior than punishment and ridicule. Many coaches tend to believe that rough, callous, or caustic treatment wins the respect of the athletes and produces the best results. This is simply not true. It is a common belief in athletics that unpleasantness and pain are more effective than pleasure and reward. All too often the yelling and scowling which follow errors are more for the coach's emotional release than for the good of the individual athlete. In fact, in some instances this approach is instrumental in alienating the athlete. It is as if the athlete feels that the coach's anger is being vented at his expense. The coach must continue to build confidence in the athlete by commending him when he makes improvement. The emphasis should be placed on the *correct* method of execution and not on the faults to be avoided.

Some athletes who have a strong desire for recognition will continue to make errors in order to have the coach continue to recognize them. If the athlete does well, the coach ignores him; if the athlete does poorly, the coach gets on his back immediately. The athlete feels that any recognition is better than no recognition at all. As a result, he will continue to make errors or even act foolishly. The coach may reverse the procedure with such athletes by simply removing them when they do poorly without any further interaction. However, when the athlete does well, the coach should give him immediate recognition. This procedure will take just a short time to become effective. In this way, the need to be recognized will be handled in a productive and not a destructive way.

PRACTICING THE TECHNIQUES

Drills The athletes must be eager to improve their skills, and a sense of accomplishment should accompany their efforts in practice. A well-planned practice is meaningful and interesting. If the team's goals are to be reached, the practice should incorporate competitive games, individual challenges, some fun, and intense effort to achieve meaningful goals which the athletes understand and with which they agree.

After being given an adequate period of time to observe, study, and experiment with techniques, the next step is to drill the performer in the motor skills. To make these skills automatic and mechanical, they must be practiced in an intelligent way.

Organizing the material in a systematic manner increases the efficiency of a drill. Disorderly approaches to the establishment of motor habits will reduce their effectiveness and increase the time required for them to become habitual. This is the reason why most coaches carefully divide the time in a practice session to include the various parts of offense and defense.

Preparation for an opponent must emphasize work on those skills which will be brought into play in the contest. This is the reason for scouting reports. If a team knows that their opponent's strength lies in their pressing defense, that must become the focus of attention in practice prior to the game. The more recently the team has practiced a skill the more effective it will be.

If a person does not continue to practice the motor skills, he may forget much of what he has learned. If, however, what he has learned is repeated enough times, it will reduce the chances of that skill being forgotten easily. *Overlearning*, therefore, means continuing well beyond the number of times it takes to learn a skill or a play. It might take fifteen minutes for a player to learn a play, but if two hours are spent learning it, rehearsing it, going through it back-

wards, forwards, and upside down, the play is not likely to
be forgotten. Once they become automatic, the moves can
be made without the player even having to think about
what he is doing. He can be executing a skill and be thinking
about something else at the same time.

Driving an automobile or using a typewriter are examples of overlearning, because both activities can become
automatic. In time, a person can talk to others, listen to
music, or even daydream while driving or typing. This was
most certainly not the case in the beginning, but by overlearning the skills of something like driving or typing, they
soon present no problem at all.

For overlearning to take place, a skill must be practiced the same day it is learned and practiced frequently
after that for a period of several weeks. Coaches must remember this when planning for the season. The coach must
also consider the fact that teams that run a minimal amount
of offense and keep the defensive assignments simple may
have an advantage over the team that uses extremely complex systems of play or styles of attack. They have the
advantage of being able to overlearn their assignments, because they are relatively simple and require a shorter practice time. Teams who have a great many plays may have the
advantage of surprise occasionally, but there is also a
greater probability of mistakes or forgotten assignments
because of the complexity of the plays. Of course, the best
situation is to have the time to overlearn complex systems
of play or styles of attack, but the coach should remember
that such an approach requires a great deal of time.

Game tempo   After the skills have been properly learned,
they *must* be practiced at game tempo. If not, the players
may form habits contrary to what is required for success in
the real situation. The coach should discourage anything but
an all-out performance from the players during drill work.
It would almost be better to terminate practice than to
continue to work with athletes who are not involved enough
to be willing to expend maximum effort. To practice poorly
means that material must be unlearned.

Length and distribution of practice sessions The length
and complexity of the practice will depend on the sport and
the interest span of the athletes, but several additional factors must be considered.

Learning takes place more efficiently during short practice periods spread over a long period of time. All coaches
feel they are fighting time. There is always something
to be covered, and there never seems to be enough time to do
it. A perennial problem facing coaches is the overlapping of
sport seasons where athletes from another sport come out
"late." This situation does not allow for the proper amount
of practice periods and often prevents proficiency of play
until mid-season. In an attempt to make up time, coaches
occasionally go too fast in their instruction, jam too much
material into short periods of time, practice too long, or do
not provide adequate time for the perfection of skills. By
doing this, the coach may begin to lose the attention of the
players. He must keep his eyes open for restlessness and
signs of disinterest. It is at this point that a minimum
amount of learning takes place. The players may develop a
sense of futility if they are given too much to learn at any
one time.

Early in the season, short practice periods close together may be effective, while a skill is being learned. This
is the reason why many coaches employ double sessions during the first two or three weeks of practice.

The amount of inactive instruction taking place on the
field of play should be very short. The greatest amount of
talking and explaining should take place indoors during
meetings. Actual demonstration is best on the field of play,
but the amount of surrounding stimuli may be so great that
it is difficult to keep the player's attention if he is not active.
The coach should try to do his teaching where there is a
minimum amount of outside stimulation. That is why it is so
very difficult to get the team's attention before the game or
at half time. There are just too many things impinging on
their attention to have accurate communication. Teaching
during competition is probably the least effective approach.
If the coach must do so, he should look directly into the

player's eyes, have him repeat the instruction, and, if possible, have him demonstrate what has been communicated.

Organization is the key to interest. If time in practice
is being spent without purpose, then there may be rapidly
diminishing returns after a certain period of time, but if
the practice is very well organized and the players know
what is scheduled along with the goals they are trying to
accomplish, then the time will seem short. Some practices
become very tiresome, simply because the athletes have no
idea how long they are going to be required to stay. Sometimes when the coach gets angry, he may extend the practice as a means of punishment. This may lead to boredom
and a loss of enthusiasm. The coach should remember that
it is not so much the length of time spent, but the quality
of the activities within the time period that makes the difference. Inactivity on anyone's part creates a feeling that
time is being wasted, and this means boring practices.
Super-organization directed toward meaningful goals will
eliminate most of this.

REFINING THE TECHNIQUES

Evaluation and self-criticism   Experience involves adjusting or adapting to the situation. As a player gains experience,
he learns to choose the correct procedure to accomplish his
goals. If the individual has participated in the solution of
the problem, his experience will be more significant than if
he was totally manipulated by an autocratic coach. Discussion, self-evaluation, and player involvement in team procedures will help to achieve the desired result.

Mental rehearsal   Some people believe that mental rehearsal will help a player execute his skills more efficiently. Some
basketball coaches have achieved excellent results by having
their players mentally practice free throw shooting. There
is no clear cut evidence that mental rehearsal is effective,
but it does, however, help the person concentrate and become
more familiar with a situation. "Skull sessions" and chalk

talks accomplish essentially the same thing. It may be of great value to encourage the players to think through novel situations which may arise. It may help them to react more rapidly and intelligently during competition.

Creativity and free play   A common technique used by many coaches to have players become acquainted with other positions is to allow free play or games in which athletes play positions very different from their own. A basketball center may play a guard position; a tight-end may get a chance at fullback or halfback. Such free play allows the player to become acquainted with the problems of another position. This interchanging of positions may be valuable later when the two athletes might have to work together. Another advantage of such play is that it may be responsible for stimulating greater feelings between team members and may increase team cohesion as well as communication. More often than not it provides an excellent release from the tensions and pressures that are often common during the season.

The coach must accept the fact that during the game he is really just an observer. At times there is very little that he can do once the game has begun. His role is very limited. He can substitute players, listen to observers, and try to make changes, but if there has not been adequate preparation before game time, the coach is virtually powerless to change the inevitable result. This places the coach in an extremely helpless position, and is the reason why so many become frustrated and emotional. They want to do something, but they are totally at the mercy of past preparation. As a result some yell, some scream, some get angry— even violent—and yes, some even cry in an attempt to make some contribution during the game. But the strings which have controlled the players up to this point have been cut and only appropriate pre-game preparation and sound techniques of instruction will help alleviate the coach's apprehension.

[handwritten margin note: not totally true. — he's not a teacher, but he's definitely not just an observer.]

chapter **10**

OUTSIDE INFLUENCES ON THE ATHLETE

Separating internal motivation from the external influences, which are present to some degree in every athlete's environment, is a difficult task. Inherent needs are hard to measure, because they are largely the products of widely diversified forces that are not easily identified.

Outside influences may be positive or negative. More often than not, they will be positive and may serve to highly motivate the athlete. If the coach can determine what these positive influences are, he may be able to arrange for their presence to a greater extent. On the other hand, if a talented athlete is failing, the coach will want to determine as early as possible if it is due to detrimental influences. Once the negative influence is identified, the coach can begin to work to remove it. The following are outside influences, which may affect the athlete either positively or negatively: parents, other family members, girlfriend, wife, teammates, press, fans, and teachers.

PARENTS

Parents are the first and usually the most direct source of outside influence on the athlete. Parental influence will differ, depending upon myriad things, as for example, the section of the country they are from, socioeconomic situation, race, religion, intelligence, education, family background, personal experience with athletics. The possibilities that may arise are too numerous and too complicated to permit a complete delineation of them.

First, the coach should be aware of the fact that participation in athletics by a son is an anxiety-provoking situation for most parents. It will help the coach if he knows how parents feel about their child's participation in athletics. Some parents will be very anxious about their son's participation in a sport like football, because of the possibility of injury. This is particularly true in fatherless homes. The mother is likely to be quite concerned over the potential loss of her son. Secretly, she does not want the boy to compete, but she allows him to participate, because she feels it may make him care more for her. Other parents may not want their son to play because it is a nuisance for them. These are selfish people, and they place their needs first. They believe that if their son becomes active in sports, chores or duties will not be taken care of. At the other extreme, some parents push the boy to compete. There may be a long line of successful athletes in their family, and they expect the boy to perpetuate the line.

Many parents have never been able to work out their apprehensions about teachers. They will see the coach as a teacher and an authority figure—a feeling that can, in itself, lead to some problems. Other parents may see the coach taking from them something that is very dear to them. They become almost jealous of the role the coach will play. He is about to become a close companion and friend to their son, a relationship they may not have enjoyed for a long time.

Some will feel the coach is in a position to give their son what they never had the opportunity to provide. A few will even resent their son having something they never had themselves.

Negative Parental Influence

It would be impossible to describe all the reasons for parental problems, but the most common bases for negative parental influences are:

The parents may feel that their son's performance reflects their child-rearing methods. They expect the child to do well. Any reflection on his play is a reflection on them also. If the person is seen as a poor player, they think they are poor parents.

Parents may attempt to fulfill their desires through their child. One of the most common attitudinal difficulties to be faced is the one in which the parents, by word or action, express the desire to obtain for their child what they never had themselves. This might be labeled the "Little League Syndrome." Parents who live out their desires through their children sometimes do irreparable damage to the child's personality. At an early age it is a natural desire on the part of the child to please the parents by doing well in an area selected for him by the parents. He sees them deeply involved in the contest, often acting in an emotional way, and this creates a serious feeling of anxiety when he knows he must succeed to please them.

Parents feel their child does poorly to punish them. Closely related to the previous problem is the attitude that the boy should want to please his parents. If he does poorly, they feel it is because he does not like them. The boy actually may be punished by the parents for doing poorly. In some cases, where this feeling is present in the parents, the boy may in fact *do* poorly as a means of punishing them. In this situation, the coach must provide a great deal of support and carefully explain to the player the basis for his actions.

Parents may use poor performance as an excuse for punishment. There are those parents who will use the athlete's poor performance as an excuse for punishing him, because they simply do not like him. They use his failure as an excuse for making him suffer. This sets him up to do poorly next time, and the cycle begins again.

Parents may reinforce negative behavior. It is even more possible that a player will do poorly to receive recognition. The more of a problem he is, the more attention he gets, and the more concerned his parents are with him. When this happens the parents are reinforcing negative behavior, because the player is getting the attention he needs when he does poorly. The parents should reverse the procedure and give him attention only when he does well.

Child's problems with parents may be displaced to athletics. A player may be working out problems he has with his parents, but it is being done through the coach. The boy really may be rebelling against the father, but since he lacks the courage to direct his anger at his father, he directs it instead at the father substitute—the coach. If there are unresolved feelings at home, the coach is likely to receive the brunt of the trouble. The boy may feel and say, "Everything is fine at home. It's this rotten basketball team that's all screwed up!"

Parents may be jealous of the child–coach relationship. If there is a close positive relationship between the father and the son, often the athlete can not decide with whom his loyalty should lie. He becomes torn between the father and the coach. If he begins to really like the coach, then he has to admit that the father may not be totally correct about everything. The father, in turn, could resent all the encouragement given the player by the coach, even though it may always be positive. Mature fathers are quick to see any conflict and will often support the coach very strongly to relieve any anxiety that may result from the conflict. On the other hand, immature or neurotically jealous fathers may intensify the conflict and cause the boy even more anxiety. The coach may deal with extreme cases by having the father feel more a part of the team. Methods of doing this appear later in the chapter.

Parental Support

It should be made clear once again that the large majority of parental influences will be positive and there is a high probability that if there is a healthy relationship between the parents and their son, there will be a good relationship between the coach and the player.

A few general procedures are recommended to help the coach avoid difficulties with parents:

1. Include the parents as much as possible in a direct and objective way.
2. Reassure the parents that, in your professional judgment, the individuals are being handled in the most effective way possible.
3. Be emphatic with the things the parents are worrying about.

All of these may be best communicated in a parents' meeting. The coach may send out letters inviting the parents to a meeting where he will explain the team rules and objectives, his personal philosophy as coach, the strategic planning which has taken place, and a brief evaluation of the team's potential. It must be emphasized that the parents should be *invited* to attend and not coerced in any way. Definite limits must be clearly stated in the letter regarding the amount of time to be spent and the subjects to be discussed. The coach must clearly emphasize that individuals and personalities will not be discussed.

During the meeting it is important for the coach to impress upon the parents the following:

1. Emphasize that the parents are a part of the team. Their cooperation and understanding are essential for success.
2. Assure the parents that the boys are in good hands and try to alleviate some of their fears regarding competition.
3. Inform the parents that every attempt will be made to handle their son as an individual. Explain that the players' best interests will serve as the basis for the decisions to be made during the season.

The coach may want to state that he in no way wishes to preempt the rights of the parents. His greatest desire is to help the boy become a successful person by coaching him in the most effective way possible.

Most parents would like to be involved in some way in the handling of their child in all areas of life, or at least be *aware* of the techniques of handling. For this reason it might be wise for the coach to provide a brief justification for his points of view. He can briefly explain why they are going to use a particular style of attack, or how they will attempt to accomplish the team goals. There is no need for the coach to feel threatened if the parents ask questions, *providing* the questions concern procedures and not players' performances.

Perhaps a social period should follow the discussion to allow parents to meet each other and the coach. It should also be quite short. Some parents will use this time to talk about their son if the coach does not set limits.

If there is enough direct communication with parents throughout the season, it is unlikely that there will be serious problems between the parents and the coach, but invariably, in spite of what the coach does to avoid it, there will be problem parents who insist on their boy playing, who punish their boy at home, and who continue to harass the coach through the season. If this happens, the coach may be forced to rely on confrontation. He can make an appointment with them, assure them that what will be discussed is in the strictest of confidence, and then just tell them exactly what he feels about the situation. He must tell them that he is doing his very best and then give them specific limits for future behavior.

OTHER FAMILY MEMBERS

The athlete may feel that he has to live up to the reputation of another family member—an uncle, a cousin, or a brother. What may be good-natured kidding about his ability by other family members may, in fact, be a considerable threat to the athlete. A talented brother's reputation, for example, may be a source of pressure to him, because other people continue to draw comparisons between the two. By referring to a player profile sheet (see Chapter 3, p. 49), the coach may become aware of this possibility. If it exists he should make an effort to support the athlete by saying, "I know you feel compelled to be as good as your brother, but please understand that you are a unique individual yourself. I only expect you to do your best and live up to your potential. I ask no more of you."

GIRLFRIEND

The girlfriend may be a much greater influence than the coach realizes. She may be not only a confidant of the athlete, but also a major source of his inspiration and motivation. It is essential, then, that the coach know something about her relationship to the player, and the influence she exerts.

To begin with, the coach might examine his own feelings about his players having girlfriends. Does he ever feel resentful toward the athlete for spending time away from the sport? Has he ever attempted to separate the two or to alienate the girl in any way?

The girlfriend of an athlete is called upon to make many sacrifices. Her boyfriend's free time is limited during the season, and he is often tired and restricted by team rules. Most girls will be understanding and help to support the player, but some will feel cheated and react in a manner which is upsetting to the athlete. The following lists a few causes for a girlfriend's discontent:

The girl may resent the sport because it takes her boyfriend away from her. She works in subtle ways to restrict his participation in the sport and to direct his interests along new lines.

The girlfriend may receive a vicarious feeling of failure if the athlete is unsuccessful. By association, if the athlete loses, she also loses some of her standing in the school. It is easy to see how the girlfriend of the star athlete becomes more important and more recognized when her boyfriend succeeds. By the same token, when a player fails, the girl may also receive a sense of failure. It hurts her prestige, and she may punish him.

The girlfriend may try to fulfill her desire for success through the athlete. In some cases, the girl may be responsible for pushing the athlete toward harder work, because she too wishes to succeed. In this case, even off the field, the player finds no release from the stress he is under.

The coach should become acquainted with the girlfriend for many reasons. She may help to provide him with a clue to the type of player with whom he is working. If she is stable, strong, and enthusiastically cooperative, there is a good chance that the athlete will be of a similar type. Dominant girls, weak girls, girls who need the limelight—all these different types will exert a different influence, or suggest the presence of a different type of athlete.

In any event, it will help if the coach shows understanding for the girlfriend. He should make a point of speaking to her around campus and perhaps comment about how tough it must be to make the sacrifices she is called upon to make.

Perhaps the best move a coach can make is to suggest to the player that he give his girl a copy of the rules and regulations so that she may be a little more understanding of his position. The coach might point out that membership on a team will mean a lot of sacrifice by both the player and the girlfriend. He may then set aside a time when the girls are allowed to come to practice.

WIFE

It is obvious that the wife will have a stronger hold on the individual than the girlfriend, but perhaps will provide no greater influence or inspiration. It is likely that their relationship will be more solid and their goals more realistic. She will be much more apt to fear his being injured and may not want him to participate. Because the wife is more concerned with security, she will be quite anxious each season about her husband's status. The sports world is a very insecure world and, even though there is a great deal of prestige involved in being married to an athlete, the wife is subject to all the fears and anxieties which are a part of the world of sport.

TEAMMATES

The athletic scene presents a large number of opportunities for creating lasting friendships. It may also lead to a number of conflicts between individuals or groups. Players on the same team, thrown together through competition, naturally tend to become close. Living and working together for an extended period of time leads to the formation of cohesive groups that are reluctant to admit a newcomer. The "rookies" are required to win the respect and the acceptance of the established veterans, and they are eager to do what they can to become a member of the select group. In spite of the trauma this situation may cause for some of the rookies, it is generally a healthy tradition, providing it does not interfere with the individual athlete's effectiveness and, at the same time, providing it stays within the rules and regulations set down by the coach. If, for any reason, the coach feels the athlete's performance is suffering as a result of the treatment he is receiving from other teammates, or if the coach feels that the treatment is seriously jeopardizing the team's unity, he must take action to stop it. As an example, every team has its "fall guy"—that person who provides the comic relief. If this person takes the kidding well and is also able to dish it out, there will probably be no problem, and it will help to bring the team together. The athlete actually looks forward to it, knowing it is a means of gaining recognition. If, however, the kidding is not of a good-natured sort—if the person is being laughed *at* and ridiculed—animosity and dissension may result.

The coach should make it very clear from the beginning that he will tolerate no behavior that humiliates any of his players. A player whom he observes suffering this humiliation should be reassured of the coach's position and thoroughly supported.

This may be a good place to mention the element of *humor*. There are many reasons why humor is important to a team. It serves as a release from tension, it builds a common bond between players, and it helps to make the obstacles less awesome. In these instances, it is *constructive*. It may also be *destructive*. It may be aimed *at* people to a degree they cannot tolerate. Finding a scapegoat may serve to boost the nervous majority's ego, but it is not the kind of thing that leads to healthy *team* unity. For one thing, most of the players are glad they are free from their teammates' barbs and secretly fear the possibility of becoming the target. This, in itself, leads to more stress.

Constructive humor involves athletes laughing at themselves. They *share* its pleasure, rather than fear its sarcastic bite. Long after their competitive days are over, the moments of humor they shared will remain uppermost in their memory.

Humor on the part of the coach can be a very effective tool. For example, rather than punishing a team for a loss, the coach may find it far more beneficial to get his point across humorously by saying something like, "We have an offense that is so proud of its defense that they gave the ball away four times. Now I admire this kind of faith, but I think we may be carrying it a bit too far."

It is not being suggested that the coach attempt to become a comedian or in any way strain to find the humor in a situation and, in doing so, act artificially. It is only suggested that if he "reads" undue stress in his players' behavior, it might help for him to relieve a little of this pressure by introducing at least a token amount of levity.

PRESS

The press needs to be understood because it comprises influential critics of the team. The attitudes of sportswriters have been instrumental in making and breaking a number of athletes and teams through the years. They have also been indirectly involved in deciding the outcome of a number of athletic contests. The expression "The pen is mightier than the sword" holds true in athletics the same as in other areas.

An important thing to keep in mind is the fact that sportswriters are human. They have needs like everyone else and are attempting to do a job in the best way they know how. Many are excellent critics of the game. They have a genuine love of the sport and fully appreciate a good performance or a game well played, regardless of the result. Some are frustrated athletes and may resent the player for having something they would like. They vindicate themselves by being critical of others. Pointing out the shortcomings of the athletes gives them a sense of importance. Others may be misplaced and are in an area they do not enjoy. Somewhere along the line they were misdirected and now find themselves involved in an activity they dislike. As a result, they have become resentful toward the assignment and toward those engaged in the activity. Such critics often view athletes as "animals," or persons of lesser intelligence and ability. They tend to report sports events in the same way. These individuals do not provide a service to the athletes or to the coach. They do a great disservice to both professions.

In all fairness to the sportswriters, they are often worked over by the athletes and the coach who fear what they write. Some coaches are intentionally unfriendly toward sportswriters or stay away from them completely, because they distrust them and are overly anxious about their influence. A general antagonism builds up between them and both lose a valuable ally. Sportswriters *are* the link between the coach and the general public, and they should be a part of the coach's plan in the same way as any motivational device. Alienating them does not help anyone in the long run.

The coach can use the press to motivate or to punish his team in an abstract way. He may be quoted as saying "This is a great team. If it would get off its duff and learn how to hit, we could be a championship ball club." Without mentioning names he has brought the problem out into the open for the team to read. The people guilty of not hitting will understand and hopefully react to it. A compliment through the press is also an outstanding form of motivation for the player. "Jones really played an outstanding game. His work has been responsible for our improvement lately." This type of simple comment can be enormously important to most players. The coach can also communicate to the *team* by means of the press. He can get an idea across to them that he may not have been able to successfully communicate before. "Tradition in our school is tremendously important and these guys have an obligation to uphold it. I think they have what it takes, but only time will tell if they want it as badly as our great teams of the past."

The press can help to build an *image*. Players may come to believe what the newspapers or magazines say about them and even help fulfill the prophesy. Coaches should be careful not to say anything in the presence of sportswriters which may be misinterpreted or which may be used by an opponent as a battle cry. Something that might have been only a side comment by a player or a coach may be expanded by the sportswriter and made to become an issue in a future contest. Whether it is done intentionally or inadvertently is hard to know, but nevertheless some teams may become very fired up by what they read in the paper.

After a loss, a coach might say something he would ordinarily not say. In his emotional state he may express certain things about the players, the team, or the opponent that may cause a great deal of difficulty when it is read by them at a later time. Even though he has second thoughts about what he said, he has no way of taking it back, and he may live to regret it later. His only remaining "out" would be to apologize directly to the team for his actions.

Sportswriters should be aware of the power they wield and the influence they exert over fans, competitors, and coaches. The coach and the press will need to work out a balance of feelings. They must respect each other's responsibilities. They must know what the limits are with each other. With most coaches there is a tendency toward including the press on almost all occasions, but they also insist that there are certain limits the press must respect, such as complete privacy for the team immediately before the contest, at half time, and immediately after the game. During practices they are allowed freedoms which do not interfere with instruction or play. The sportswriter must have some respect for the position the coach is in. He should not expect a coach to give him the inside, secret information on an upcoming game or to be ready to say things that will build a controversy. If the sportswriter honors the coach's position and the coach fully understands the significant influence of the press, there should be no major problems.

FANS

It is necessary in discussing outside influences to give serious consideration to the importance of the fan. The world of sports could hardly survive without him, and yet the fan can produce mixed feelings on the part of the athlete.

On the positive side, the fan can offer the support so sorely needed at crucial times. There is perhaps nothing so warming, comfortable, and supportive as a bleacher full of individuals spurring the athlete on to do his very best. Some sections of the country and some cities are famous for the strong support given the team. In some cities, the entire season is sold out well in advance and to get a ticket to a game is considered an extreme privilege. Such fans are extremely loyal. There is no doubt as to the "good" guy and the "bad" guy. Playing under such circumstances can be an inspirational event and can help the athlete put out an extra amount of effort. For the opponent, it can be an intimidating encounter, one which he would prefer to avoid. This extremely positive feeling can be a large source of motivation, since the athlete can feel respected and appreciated for his efforts.

In other instances, the number of fan clubs for athletes can be a great source of motivation and inspiration. Athletes who are singled out to be honored can have a sense of security, knowing that someone or some group is concerned with their welfare and has taken special effort in singling them out as special people. In these instances, the backing and support provide a great motivational force.

During the actual athletic contest, the fans can prove to be a great inspiration at particularly crucial times. The extra backing can be of great value particularly to the athlete who is concerned about what others think of him. By performing before others and being appreciated by them, he is able to show he is worthwhile.

Fans follow teams for many different reasons. Going to the game serves some need for them. They may go for enjoyment, relaxation, or just to see a team that they have had the opportunity to view on television, hear about on the radio, or read about in the newspapers. At times, they may go simply to be entertained without any involvement.

On the negative side, there are those fans who remain loyal only if their team wins. If the team loses or is mediocre, they are quick to turn on the team. There are even some people who attend games from a totally negative standpoint. Their fun comes from seeing the home team lose. Failure in others means a kind of success for them. The herd instinct is very strong during athletic contests and many people find themselves caught up in an emotional fervor, which sometimes leads to highly immature behavior.

No matter how much an athlete tells you he does not hear the fans, there will be times he cannot escape their influence. His degree of sensitivity has a lot to do with it, but the close proximity of the fans in most sports make it impossible to shut them out completely. Of course, the biggest target everywhere is the player who is performing poorly, but even outstanding players are prime targets for the opposing team's fans. Many players feel an intense obligation to perform for the fans and are quite disappointed when they do not succeed. They try so hard to excel that the desire actually interferes with the execution of the skill.

A few players perform even better when the fans are for the other team. The rebellious athlete who is aggressive and assertive is in his element. What would destroy a show-off makes him feel right at home. Some athletes play much better at home—they need the support and feel much more comfortable. Sites away from home can present a serious challenge to players because of the reception. In an intense rivalry situation, if the coach knows his players will face a hostile reception, he should discuss the matter with them and explain what they should expect. He would want the team to keep close and face the potential danger together. He also must prevent his own troublemakers from causing trouble by telling them exactly how he feels about their conduct and what penalties will be imposed if they behave inappropriately. Most importantly, the players should be convinced of the fact that the place to beat the opponent is on the field of play.

The coach should have a definite plan to follow in getting his own fans involved. Essentially, he should be concerned with their needs and do what he can to make them feel more a part of the activity. This would include giving the fans a symbol of identification. Pins, buttons, pennants, etc., help to make a person identify more readily with a team and, in so doing, support and defend it. Half time entertainment is provided for the enjoyment of the fans. Fan appreciation nights, wildly gay routines by bands, cheerleaders, and song girls, drawings, autographed pictures or balls, and having the athletes work during the off-season or during the summer in a public-relations capacity all have their place in creating public interest and support.

A difficult responsibility for some coaches to assume is speaking at rallies or at booster group meetings. He invariably mentions fan support. It has become somewhat ritualistic during the speech for the coach to say that he wants the fans to come out and support the team, because it will help them win. This is a rather trite statement which has been heard for many years. Like anything else, his comments about the fans and their support needs some forethought and some planning. It might be more effective if he were to actually set up a challenge situation between his school's rooting section and the other school's section. "There are few rooting sections or schools who show better support than our opponent. They are extremely vocal and well organized. Our team has accepted the challenge. Now, how about you accepting the challenge? You're part of this team. We represent you and we expect an effort on your part just as you expect an outstanding effort on our part!"

If the coach sees this as just a chore or a duty, it will very likely come off poorly. But an effective approach with the fans may lead to more effective play by the members of the team, so the time spent is well worth it. He must also be very careful to congratulate the fans for an outstanding show if they performed well. It's much like recognizing a player. They will be back again, more eager than ever.

TEACHERS

Teachers are important outside influences on the athlete in one very significant way. They hold the key to a player's eligibility. If the coach has the other faculty members' approval, he may receive the courtesy of having them report on a player's progress in class. With this information, the coach may be able to avoid a player's ineligibility by seeing to it that the athlete improves his study habits in conformance with the teacher's suggestions. Since some teachers exert a considerable influence on their students, it is to be hoped that the teacher will hold a favorable opinion of both the athletic program and the coach in charge. The coach would be wise to communicate his intentions of working in harmony with the teacher to establish a program of assistance for the young man so that he not only will be able to keep his grades up in his regular classes, but also will be eligible for athletics.

It is always to the coach's advantage to know what the outside influences on his players are and to what degree they affect the players' performances. This information may provide the coach with better avenues of approach in understanding the athlete and his problems.

chapter 11

CULTURAL AND MINORITY PROBLEMS

One of the coach's major responsibilities in dealing with
all athletes is to provide them with an equal opportunity to
demonstrate their ability under equal conditions. Every
athlete, regardless of his race, color, creed, or religion,
would like to feel that he is being assessed primarily on his
talent. If a player feels he is being evaluated for any other
reason, it not only will interfere with his performance, but
also may cause him to use his talent to get back at the
coach, particularly if he is an immature athlete.

If possible, to help insure greater harmony on the
team, the coach should make an effort to justify his selection of players as objectively as possible. Any form of evidence—statistics, charts, films, or tests—will provide the
players with a basis for understanding and accepting the
coach's decisions. This is not to say that this information
will *satisfy* the athletes or lead them to accept the coach's
decision without question, but it will certainly help. This is
also not intended to suggest that statistics or tests will *always* be the best basis for player selection. For example,
there are some athletes who perform much better under
game conditions than they do in practice or vice versa.

Usually, this fact *can* be borne out statistically. If not, the coach should justify his decisions by explaining his evaluation and saying that in his estimation the players he has selected are the ones best qualified to do the job in the game.

Although the coach should make an effort to treat each player fairly, there is something that is even more important. The coach must focus on and attempt to use the individual trait that makes the player perform at his maximum potential. Each player has a special "button" to be pushed that may make him a winner. What is done with one player will not necessarily work with another. Unfortunately, this "different" treatment is often interpreted by some as a lack of fairness on the coach's part.

PROBLEM AREAS AND ATTITUDES

As citizens our birthright provides that we are free and equal human beings, but it would be a mistake to treat the players on the team as equal personalities. The player should know his rights immediately, because everyone's will be the same, but each player must also receive a feeling of being unique. The coach must try to deal with each individual on the basis of his personality traits. This idea should not be too difficult for the coach to accept, but it may be extremely difficult to *do*. For example, a basketball coach who has been a guard is comfortable working with other guards. He understands their problems; he knows their moves; he is aware of the strategy from that position. With the "big men"—the forwards and the centers—he may be quite uncomfortable. Never having played the position himself, he may not really understand all the intricacies of that assignment. In short, he does not "think" like a "big man" so he has trouble dealing with one. He must become completely familiar with the position before he can meaningfully empathize with those players. The same problem exists to an extent in working with personality types. A middle-class white basketball coach can probably understand a middle-class white basketball player. It may be very difficult for him to understand a black athlete from the ghetto. Just as the coach must learn to empathize and communicate with the big man to be successful, so must he learn to empathize with the special characteristics of all his athletes.

The coach must build a firm philosophy about athletes from different cultural groups. This cannot be done without involvement in that cultural group. Since the coach is often a recognized and respected member of the community, the most obvious way he may understand the basic philosophies of cultural groups is to become involved in community ethnic affairs. A coach can become more effective if he is aware of the needs of the community which he serves.

The coach should be acutely aware of the fact that there are certain cultural differences between various groups. To be successful with any of these groups, he must understand their differences. In some groups, for example, there may be different rituals, special forms for expressing respect, and certain reactions that are responsible for the player's behavior or responses. The player may be responding as he is expected to respond within his cultural group. Often coaches react negatively to certain types of behavior, because they do not recognize these behavior patterns as being indigenous to the given culture. They attribute the motivations for these characteristics to negative influences. These attitudes occur for the same reason there have been problems between people of different backgrounds for centuries—fear of something that is unfamiliar (xenophobia).

Fear of a cultural group manifests itself in a number of strange ways. The stereotyped characteristics attributed to certain cultures may influence the coach's reaction toward that group. For example, it is common to attribute to a minority group traits that are considered negative or unacceptable to the majority within the culture. Nicknames and derogatory phrases often reflect these attitudes.

Few people will admit to a prejudice, but we all have our prejudices. There is someone or something each of us dislikes. Very often people rationalize their dislike for a minority group member by attributing some negative trait to him, and then disliking him because he "possesses" that

trait. People who attribute certain stereotyped characteristics to a group seem to be sensitive to and pick out from
the group only those individuals who exhibit negative traits.
It is a rather common tendency for people to attribute to
an entire group certain characteristics they have observed
in one or two members. The coach must be careful not to
assume that an entire group possesses characteristics he has
seen manifested in one athlete. It is not uncommon for
coaches to use a cultural group as a "scapegoat." Some players are blamed for all the ills of a team. In such instances,
the cultural group is given the full responsibility for the
team's lack of success. Instead of its being seen as an overall team problem to work out, it becomes "their fault."

The following is a list of problem areas or problem attitudes that may affect the relationship between a coach
and minority group athletes:

*The coach may unconsciously "set up" a self-fulfilling
prophesy.* An athlete who feels he has sufficient talent to
be on the first team is placed on the second unit by a coach
who wishes to test his willingness to work. The player may
develop the attitude, "What's the sense of trying? I don't
have a chance anyway." The player then gives up, and the
coach uses his quitting as an example of why the player
did not make it—he was lazy. In other words, the coach
predetermined that the person was lazy, put him on the second club, causing him not to perform, and, therefore, proved
his first estimate of the boy was true. The coach then points
to the situation as an example of how lazy the player is.
What may have been a good "technique" with another
player produced failure, because the coach was unaware of
the player's feelings. Had the coach known the player's feelings and had he explained the situation to him, the player's
negative response might have been avoided.

*The athlete may be frightened of belonging to a certain
cultural group.* The athlete might find it hard to believe
that the coach wants to know his background, and he might
attempt to cover up information about himself. There is a

fear of being exposed, and it produces suspicion, with-drawal, and discomfort. For example, a person who does not have any money and who comes from a ghetto may be ashamed of it. When the coach tries to get acquainted, the player may become defensive. The coach must not interpret this defensiveness as a personal affront. The player is only trying to protect his own ego-integrity.

Minority athletes may try to find something that will make them unique or different from the majority. These athletes want to have a sense of pride—something that belongs to them. The coach may find that he is frightened, disgusted, or worried about the fact that they have their particular symbol. As long as the identifying symbol does not run contrary to the team's image, as long as it does not under-mine team principles, rules, or regulations, there is no rea-son for not letting the group retain the characteristic that gives them a sense of identity. To displace individual group identities, the coach could provide the *team* with an identi-fying characteristic that all members could believe in and would adopt. This would give them a sense of pride and make them feel special. Once again, the coach should be fully aware of the philosophy of the athletes' culture; other-wise, he may misinterpret their behavior.

The coach must realize that each athlete may have a very different motivation for playing. Different reactions than the coach is accustomed to from past experience may result from various situations. For example, the athlete may not be used to handling success or may not be in tune with suc-cess. This may cause a noted change in his behavior. Even though success comes to him through athletics, he may tend to forget about the source of his success and focus only on the rewards it brings. In this case, the coach may have to assume the role of father and help the athlete develop self-control.

Some minority group athletes who have had very lim-ited success experiences find that when they become a mem-ber of a team and are placed in a relatively important position, their perspective becomes distorted. They begin to feel more important than they actually may be. They may even believe that the team really cannot do without them. As a result, they begin to defy authority and break rules. Often the successful athlete, who previously had not felt worthwhile or important, may experience a feeling of anger at having been poorly treated in the past. The star athlete—the person around whom the team is built—may even use his position to "pay back" all those people who have hurt him in the past. Formerly, he was made to feel inferior and now, in a position of superiority, he has an unconscious desire to "get even" with all those people who were responsible for the earlier discomfort. "Getting even" can be done in several ways: the athlete may become erratic in his play (he does exceptionally well at one time and poorly at another) ; he may perform only at his whim; or he may take a team all the way to a very crucial position and then perform very poorly. He may be partially aware of what he is doing, but, more than likely, it will be done unconsciously. Inwardly he feels, "You said I'd fail and that I was no good, so now it's my turn to do some hurting."

It is the coach's responsibility to help such athletes become aware of the reasons for their rebellious attitudes. If the coach is unable to do this and help the player work through his problems, the attitude is likely to continue, and the athlete will probably behave in a similar manner after he has finished with athletic competition. He will continue to defy authority and act in an angry way, particularly after having an opportunity for recognition. His success in athletics boosts his confidence and makes him more aggressive. Unfortunately, this type of immature behavior often reflects on his ethnic or racial group and provides a basis for continued criticism of that group by some people. Narrowminded observers will interpret this as a reflection on that entire culture group.

Athletes may find it difficult to adjust to new environment. When the coach is recruiting different types of athletes and he removes them from their environment, he should not expect them to leave their environmental influences behind and immediately adjust to the new situation. They will continue to be basically what they were in the old surroundings. In a number of cases this has led to considerable difficulty— either the players have been unable to adapt, or the coach has been unable to utilize the player's talents, because he does not understand, or is unwilling to accept, their standards of behavior. In truth, the coach may be responsible for the disharmony that results, because he has put the person in an alien atmosphere.

The coach must be careful not to use athletes from different cultures to show that he is not prejudiced. The coach may go overboard in protecting some athletes at the risk of losing the rest of the team. He may be either so defensive about the athlete or so frightened of losing him that he treats him in a manner that expresses favoritism to the other players. For them to see the coach refrain from chewing out the person, or to see him give the player extra privileges or special publicity will cause dissension and a feeling of hostility toward both the player and the coach. This "special" handling by the coach may be the result of his own feelings of guilt or his fearfulness about what will happen to the athlete. His trying to undo all the wrong that has been done in the past is unrealistic. It becomes unfair to the rest of the team and they will resent it. He may lose the team if he plays the person in place of someone else, simply because he wants to favor these athletes. The player, himself, will also sense it and may resent being used in this manner.

During an emotional crisis, the coach may direct his insults at a particular minority group on the other team. If this happens it may totally devastate his own team members. Many coaches have completely lost their athletes this way. The insult may have been said so fast that the coach was completey unaware of what he said. One unkind allusion to a group's characteristics at the wrong moment is all that it takes to destroy everything the team has built up in the way of mutual respect and cooperation.

*A coach may crystallize all his prejudice into his handling
of one athlete.*   One person may receive all the coach's
displaced hostility. Every weakness that the coach recognizes in others is punished in the given group member. It
would help if the coach were able to determine to what degree he is actually prejudiced. The coach should make a
personal exploration to determine his own areas of prejudice in athletics. Who are the athletes he dislikes and why?
What may be the cause of the prejudice? What can he do
about it? Although this may not be the easiest of tasks, it
can provide insights which may be helpful to him as well as
the team. Psychologically, it is more productive for a person
to be aware of his prejudices and to attempt to do something
about them rather than to deny them and have them produce
detrimental effects unknowingly. There are times when the
coach may deny or be unaware of his prejudices. In such
instances, it is important for him to listen to feedback from
others and consider it seriously rather than to deny or defend his actions. The more vigorous and vehement the denial and defensiveness, the higher the probability that the
coach harbors some prejudices which are difficult to face.
If specific behaviors are pointed out, with alternatives, this
often provides an inroad to making changes. In any case,
the coach should be aware of his own prejudicial behaviors.
This will be impossible for most, but inwardly a coach may
be able to admit to his real feelings and work them out in
a manner that is not destructive to the team.

*Prejudice can develop from outside influences of parents
and alumni.*   Parents of athletes and members of the alumni
may be responsible for a source of ill-feeling. These outside
influences must be dealt with when they begin to affect performance, but the coach will find it extremely difficult in
most cases, because both the parental influence and the
alumni pressure is indirect and subtle (although it may
become open and direct in some situations). In effect, the
coach may be putting his job on the line by holding true to
his own convictions. He should make his position very clear
to everyone from the beginning. In this way, he will be able

to meet the *critics of his policies,* not people who are using his policies as an excuse for criticism when his team loses. With parents, the coach's views can be expressed at the parents' meeting, and with the alumni, they can appear in a newsletter.

A coach may be envious of the talent of a player or players from a cultural group. The coach might prefer that the talent be found in his own group. As a result he may be resentful of a talented cultural group, and his resentment may take many forms. He may expect more from them in terms of performance. The expectation may go beyond their capabilities, but they will continually be driven because of the coach's excessive demands. The coach may be continually critical and downgrading. By placing the athlete in what is an impossible situation, the coach can feel justified in his punishment. The end result may be a feeling of futility on the athlete's part.

Another form of resentment may be the direct castigation of the player via insults, snide comments, or reprimands in front of the team. The coach may feel these actions are justified, because the athlete is not producing up to expectations. A more truthful reason would be that the coach resents the talent that the athlete possesses and would prefer that he be the gifted one. It is not uncommon in athletics for a coach who possessed minimal talent during his own career to be super-critical and overdemanding of a talented athlete on his team. It is as if he is trying to get the athlete to do all those things he was unable to accomplish when he performed. When this is the case, talented athletes pay a heavy price for being a member of the team. If they belong to a particular cultural group, the demands are even more overbearing.

A minority group athlete is usually painfully aware that he belongs to a particular cultural group. There may be a tendency for the athlete to use the fact that he is a member of a particular group as an excuse for his failure. The athlete may not have enough talent to be playing regularly and yet feel he is being slighted because of his background. Consciously or unconsciously, he views not playing as a manifestation of the coach's prejudice. This poses a most difficult problem for the coach, because the athlete is apt to guard against an objective evaluation of his performance. In such cases, the coach must try to be as objective as possible by keeping accurate records of the athlete's performance. Hopefully, this may aid the coach in helping the athlete reach an objective appraisal of his own ability.

Before the season starts, the coach must make known his position that everyone trying out for the team has equal rights and will be provided an opportunity to make the club. He can reaffirm the position that if anyone on the team is being picked on or ridiculed because of his race, creed or color, he will take whatever action necessary to deal with it effectively. By doing so, the coach will support all members of his team early and hopefully avoid potential problems.

If the problems actually do arise, the coach should take immediate action to carry out his promise. Even if the problem is only scuttlebutt, it should not be overlooked. The coach should call in the player or players responsible and say something like, "I don't know whether it's true or not, but I've heard that someone has been riding Bill pretty hard. If it *is* going on, I want it stopped immediately. I want no more remarks made which will lead to team problems. If you are guilty of this, or know of anyone who is, see to it that it's stopped before it goes any further." If members of the team are found in violation of the rules, the coach must then take immediate action by handling it the way he would any other rule infraction.

MINORITY GROUP ATHLETES
AND TEAM COHESIVENESS

There are several different coach–player relationships possible when discussing teams composed of athletes from

minority groups. Each situation will require special handling. The ideas expressed are applicable to athletes from
all different cultures.

Few minority group athletes   The coach should go to each
minority group team member individually and let him know
that he will protect him and give him an equal chance to
make the team. The coach should try to become as closely
acquainted with the cultural group as possible in order to
understand its basic philosophy. He needs to understand the
individual as well as the minority culture. His primary concern is protecting the individual.

Half minority group athletes   On a team consisting of ap-
proximately half minority group athletes, the coach needs
to confront the whole team with the fact that there is a
potential problem in the area of team cohesion. In this situation, the coach is required to know much more about the
cultural background of the minority. He still needs to protect the athletes, but there are enough minority members
to help protect each other. The coach may face a serious
problem in trying to solidify the group against outside influences. The coach should initiate and encourage team interaction on many different levels, the goal being to have
the team members better understand one another.

All minority group athletes   The coach in this case will
want to make it clear to the players that the teams they play
will present the greatest number of problems. Team cohesion will be strong, but the coach, to be successful, must
thoroughly understand the minority culture and spend a
great deal of time around the school or neighborhood to get
acquainted with the conditions and customs. In handling the
athletes, all the coach has as a frame of reference is his
own style of life and set of values. These may be completely
out of tune with the minority athlete's life and values. To
apply his standards to them is unfair. He therefore needs to
learn a great deal to be able to "speak their language." The

most effective approach might be to say, "Look, I'm not fully aware of the basis for all your motivations and needs, but I do know football. So let me be the person to decide what's right for the team. I'm going to be in charge, but I need to know what's going on. We need to work together if we're going anywhere."

The coach might meet regularly with the players to discuss the culture, the problems, the feelings and situations faced by minority group athletes. This constant contact can give the coach a greater feeling of what it would be like to be in the same situation.

When the team is composed of only a few minority group athletes, the biggest problem is handling the individual and protecting him from negative outside influences. When half the team is a minority group, the biggest threat is internal team problems. With all minority members, the coach has to worry about other teams getting on the players and affecting their play. The threat will help solidify the team. If they are already unified, it will be easy to get them together to face the outside world.

A coach dealing with a predominance of minority group athletes needs to accomplish three things with his athletes. (1) He must convince them he is an authority in that sport. There are many ways in which he can accomplish this, but none beats intelligent organization. (2) He should present the activity in a manner that is appealing and meaningful to the particular group. The coach, in fact, is in a position to give minority group athletes something that is very important to them. With some minority groups, particularly black athletes, sports represents one of the easier avenues of success available to them. Since success is attractive to them, they are actually less likely to rebel openly against the coach (subtly, perhaps). They recognize the fact that the coach can help them gain success. In minority schools, athletics often represent a rallying point, and the coach may find it effective to solidify the school around the sport. He may even become a hero in this situation. (3) He must work toward developing their trust. This will be the most difficult of the three. The approach being advocated throughout the book—understanding and treating each athlete as an individual in the areas of communication and motivation—will again produce the best results. Admittedly, this is harder and far more complex with the minority athlete than with others, because it will probably take much longer to understand the athlete who comes from a culture that is often much different from that of the coach. He must be willing to spend a great deal of time finding out about that culture.

If the coach, himself, is a member of a minority group, he may face the same three coach–player relationships, but he must approach them differently:

Few minority group athletes In dealing with a non-minority-group team, the coach should begin by stating his philosophy of handling the players on an equal basis and openly discuss the problems that might arise. The minority group player being coached by a minority group member might present the greatest problem. If the athlete feels he is being picked on, he will also feel totally defeated. The player expects to be supported, and he gets harsh treatment instead. In some cases, the coach may be trying to identify with and become a part of the majority, and he tries to do this by favoring the majority. In other instances, the coach may be picking on the athlete, because he feels the athlete should be superior to the other members. If this is the reason, he *must* tell the athlete why he is doing it. Simply saying, "I'm going to expect more from you because I think you've got more to give," will be all that is necessary. If this is not said, the player will be totally humiliated before the rest of the team, because he will feel that even someone from his own group is unwilling to protect him.

Half minority group athletes The majority group athletes may feel threatened, because they may be afraid the coach will favor the minority. Again the coach must make clear his position to the entire team. If not carefully handled, an internal team problem may arise. Two separate groups may emerge and cause serious disharmony.

All minority group athletes There will be an unspoken motivational force at work in this situation. The approach, "Here is our chance to show ourselves," can create great ambition, pride, and team spirit, but the bond that is created can also perpetuate the prejudice that there may be on the part of the minority athlete and even make it stronger. The coach must take special care to see that the racial bond does not become a "rallying cry" of the team. It may create racial barriers that do not already exist, which may add to the team's problems. He must however, take special care to prepare his athletes to withstand the various forms of abuse that may be directed at them by other teams.

SOCIAL PROTEST OR ATHLETIC COMPETITION?

In recent years, the athletic world has been rocked by minority group attacks against coaches, teams, and management. The accusations range from exploitation to discrimination, and they exist on all levels of competition in every sport. Minority group athletes, themselves, have been coerced and intimidated by their own people. Coaches have been subjected to intense pressure, and some have lost their jobs. Many schools have set up fairness committees to study minority grievances in the athletic program. Perhaps most disturbing of all, some schools and coaches who fear future problems are beginning to have reservations about recruiting minority athletes.

In few other fields have minority group members received the same degree of opportunity for recognition and success as in athletics. The best have become the idols of millions. Most professional sports include in their number a large percentage of minority group athletes. They have, in turn, used athletic participation as a springboard to embark on careers in politics, business, and the entertainment world. In short, even though these athletes had trouble cracking the barriers at first, the athletic world has provided more rewards than most other fields. This is not to suggest that the benefits have not been mutual, or that these athletes have not been used. Exploitation has certainly taken place in a number of places. But unlike other areas of endeavor, athletics have opened a number of closed doors. With few exceptions today, athletic competition is open to anyone who displays the necessary talent. However, because of the fear of the problems that can arise with minority groups, these doors may begin to close in some areas and the opportunities may begin to grow more limited. A few coaches have made the decision to stop recruiting the minority group athlete, because he does not want to put both his job and his program in jeopardy. The athlete who uses sports as a means of making known his feelings about other areas of life may find limited opportunities to speak out as coaches and schools begin to look elsewhere for talent.

It is a major dilemma that faces both the minority group athlete and the coaching profession. In reality, athletics is a narrowly circumscribed area of endeavor. By no means is it the totality of a person's existence. Although the coach should do what he can to help the cause of his minority people, in the long run his main responsibility must be to develop a successful team. That is his prime purpose. He cannot take on all the problems of mankind. He may, in fact, have to eliminate those players who interfere with his pursuit of that goal.[1]

From one point of view, the coach *is* a prejudiced person—he puts the most talented players on the field. He chooses those who are to play. He does not put people on the field because of the color of their skin, or because of their religion, or eye color, or length of hair. He puts them on the field because he thinks they will be successful. He makes a decision based on his own best judgment. Considered in its finest sense, a person should be evaluated and judged not on how he looks and acts, but on the basis of what he is and what he has to offer.

---

1. For a detailed description of the problems as viewed by the black athlete, the reader should become acquainted with the following: Edwards, H., *The Revolt of the Black Athlete* (New York: Free Press, 1969).

chapter 12
PSYCHOLOGICAL SCOUTING

To defeat an opponent, coaches earnestly strive to employ different techniques and all elements of strategy that can be devised. All teams know this and spend a great deal of time preparing for as many eventualities as possible. When a physical weakness is detected in an opponent, the coach does not hesitate to take advantage of it. He does everything he can to learn the best method of attack against an opponent and also to discover what means of attack that opponent will use against him. Hundreds of hours may be spent scouting an opponent in an attempt to uncover this information.

"Psyching out the other guy" has become a very common expression in the athletic world. "Psyching" involves picking out the psychological weaknesses of an opponent and then using these weaknesses to defeat him. Manipulating an individual by creating doubt or confusion in him is very much a part of athletics, but one that is highly unsophisticated, underdeveloped, and misunderstood by a great many coaches and athletes.

Success in athletics requires an emotional involvement. Players win because winning fills some need, makes them feel pleasurable, and provides them with an emotional outlet. The emotion cannot be denied. The player feels good when he wins and probably sad when he loses. Emotions, therefore, play a large part in winning and losing. Just as a coach develops players physically, so must he develop them psychologically. Just as he handles physical problems, so must he handle psychological problems. Psychological scouting, then, involves uncovering information about the personality strengths and weaknesses of an opponent. The coach must also be aware that strengths and weaknesses exist in his own club. An athlete who cannot "take it" psychologically has just as much of a weakness as the athlete who is devoid of talent. At the present time, however, there is no really efficient system for determining psychological weaknesses.

THE ETHICS OF PSYCHOLOGICAL GAME PLAY

Before delving too deeply into the subject, one issue must be faced. A number of coaches may seriously question the *ethics* involved in scouting for, and playing to, psychological weaknesses. In general, coaches share a great deal of information, such as techniques of play, strategy, and information on opponents. Coaching is an extremely unselfish profession. Coaches, however, are somewhat reluctant to bring "personal" information on their individual athletes out into the open, because they feel it borders on unethical behavior, or, more realistically, because no clear guidelines have ever been developed to help the coach accumulate and understand this information.

It is important to deal with the unethical issue first. To begin with, it is assumed that most coaches will behave ethically as teachers. If, in fact, the coach were guilty of scheming and contriving by using underhanded practices, it would work against him in the long run. Most of his players would come to think of him as an unscrupulous person for whom they could have no respect. Psychological scouting *must not* become a search for opportunities to use dirty tactics and must not extend beyond the field of play and into the individual's personal life.

The purpose of psychological scouting is not to destroy an *individual* any more than knocking down an opponent in football is intended to maim or seriously injure that person. It really has nothing to do with the player as a person, but rather as an opponent who has strengths to be avoided and weaknesses to take advantage of.

In a somewhat limited way, psychological "maneuvering" is being practiced by most athletes and coaches. For example, if a new defensive back comes into the game, everyone knows he will have to go through his baptism of fire. If he handles it successfully, he will not remain the prime target, but if he cannot handle himself, the opponent's attack may center on him exclusively until he is driven out of the game. Again, it is not an attempt to destroy the *individual*, but only a strategic move to defeat the opponent. The player who is attacked continuously needs handling in the area of his weakness. Handling problems or weaknesses of the individual athletes is what coaching is all about, and weaknesses are *not* limited to techniques of play. If it is learned that a particular player is emotionally unstable, it is just as much a part of the game as if he were slow or could not play defense. The coach must prepare his team psychologically, as well as technically. He should also be prepared to play to the psychological weaknesses in others when they are detected.

SCOUTING METHODS

Accumulating information on the psychological weaknesses of an athlete is a very difficult job, unless the coach knows specifically what to look for and how to use the information once it is discovered.

To begin with, the scout should be an intelligent and perceptive person who is in tune with the subtleties of human interaction. He should also be aware of the inherent strengths and weaknesses of the personality types as discussed in Chapters 2 and 3.

When scouting for technique and strategy, the person focuses on the field of play. Psychological scouting, on the other hand, focuses on sideline activity, bench conduct, or athletes before or immediately after competitive encounters. The scout must be alert before a play starts or after the play is over. He should observe the coach, bench, or concentrate on a single player for several plays, regardless of what is happening, to see how the individual or the group handles a variety of situations.

The scout should arrive in time to watch the players during warm-ups. During the warm-ups he should attempt to determine the following:

1. The personality traits of the coach. Is he close to the players or is he detached? Is he anxious about the contest? What is his attitude toward, and his relationship with, the officials when they meet? If he comes in contact with the other coach, is there any ill feeling apparent?

2. The players' feelings for each other. Are they close? Do they have a strong esprit de corps? Are they independent, divided into cliques, or one solid unit?

3. The player's attitude toward the contest. Are they relaxed and confident or are they nervous? Are they lethargic or enthusiastic? Do they seem to be working hard or do they rest and take it easy when possible?

All of these factors provide clues and may suggest what to look for in the future. Assuming a person has a particular personality trait on the basis of one observation may be a serious mistake. Several observations can lead to a detectable behaviorial pattern, and this pattern may provide the coach with meaningful information. While the game is in progress, more information should be obtained:

1. Does the coach encourage or punish his players? Does he seem to support them in times of crisis, or does he become detached during those moments?

2. When players come out of the game, do they pout at the end of the bench or do they remain enthusiastic and support their replacement? Is there interaction between

the player and other members of the team on the bench? Do they appear to be concerned solely with their own play and disinterested in the success of the team?

3. Are there players who appear to be emotionally unstable? Do they argue with the officials? Do they fight with other players? Are they good sports? Would getting them rattled help? Can the player stand pressure?

The scout should keep these general questions in mind while watching another team. A routine can be established to help the coach elicit specific information. The scout is really looking for information that will help him evaluate individual personality traits. A game plan should include an approach intended to take advantage of individual weaknesses in the opponent. Simply stated, the trait that is missing in the individual or in the team becomes the point of attack. While by no means a definitive list of what the scout should look for, Table 5 may help to provide some direction. Three things are contained in this table: the name of the trait, the behavioral manifestation observed by the scout, and the action to be taken against the observed psychological strength or weakness. The result of the scout's observations can provide a basis for the development of a pyschological game plan.

The purpose of Table 5 and the general observations is to give the coach a rough idea as to the nature of psychological scouting. It is by no means a definitive list. The coach will be able to develop his own ideas as he becomes more acquainted with this approach. He should not accept the suggested behavior outline without question. In fact, some of the observations may be related to very different traits than those suggested. It is recommended that the coach make his decisions only after a number of observations. To further insure against any errors, he might have assistants make the same observations and compare them. In any case, the more information, the better position the coach will be in to make decisions.

If an accurate file is kept on each player, the coach will begin to get a general feeling about that player and how he can be handled effectively. By working with the psycho-

TABLE 5. Nature of Psychological Scouting

Trait	Behavior Observed	Psychological Game Plan
	High	
	1. Claps hands when he or teammate does well.	Should be matched against an equally hard working and determined athlete.
	2. Slams ball down and shows more desire immediately after.	Do not challenge him. Recognize him as being good. The challenge will bring out the best in him.
	3. Enthusiastic, hard worker during warm-ups.	
Drive	4. Does best against tough opponent.	
	Low	
	1. Plays best against poor teams.	Put him under pressure early in game.
	2. Shows little enthusiasm during warm-ups and game.	Do everything possible to beat him early because he will have a tendency to fold.
	High	
	1. First on field or court in warm-ups.	Needs to be matched against hard-working, dedicated athlete.
	2. Last off field or court during warm-ups.	
	3. Runs to position rather than walks or jogs.	
Determination	4. Works extra hard on his own.	
	Low	
	1. Last on field or court during warm-ups.	Work hard on this athlete early in the game, and he will tire late in the game.
	2. Goes through assignments routinely.	

	High	
	1. Slams ball down, becomes more aggressive.	Need to match him against your toughest, most aggressive athlete. Condition the players to face aggression. Lead him into situation where he will lose his temper.
	2. Refuses to shake hands, ignores opponent.	
	3. Continues pushing after whistle.	
	4. Gets penalties for offensive and aggressive fouls.	
	5. Starts fights or fouls obviously.	
Aggression	Low	
	1. Congratulates aggressive opponents.	Pour on the aggression early in the game, and he will fold under it.
	2. Stops before whistle.	
	3. Accepts penalties without question or complaint.	
	4. Is quick to serve as peacemaker in times of anger between teams.	
	High	
Leadership	1. Talks to officials or even yells at them when a bad call occurs.	A hard, tough, mature person is needed to handle him.
	2. Asks questions of coach and even, on occasion, talks back to him.	
	3. Tells other players what to do.	
	4. Yells from bench.	
	5. Encourages other players.	

TABLE 5. (Continued)

Trait	Behavior Observed	Psychological Game Plan
Leadership (continued)	**Low**	
	1. Rarely communicates with officials or openly questions calls.	Attempt to intimidate. Does not handle pressure well. In periods of stress, direct attack at him.
	2. Remains somewhat in the background when around others—interested, perhaps, but usually as an observer.	
	3. Listens to the coach, but usually does not talk back or question his dictates.	
Coachability	**Uncoachable**	
	1. Avoids looking at coach when the coach is talking to him.	Attempt to force this athlete to make a mistake early in the game. This would lead to handling by the coach and a possible conflict between the two.
	2. Folds arms when talking to the coach or is preoccupied with other matters.	
	3. Turns back on coach or stays completely away from him during the game.	
Emotional Stability	**Stable**	
	1. His play seems to get better as the pressure grows greater.	Do not overexert yourself against him early in the game in an attempt to rattle him. It just won't work. Stick to a steady game plan and work on him gradually.
	2. Does not show excitement during critical periods—interest, but not much emotion.	
	3. Bad calls by officials do not affect him. May even make him do better.	

Emotional Stability (continued)	**Unstable**	Put a great deal of pressure on this athlete early to disrupt his game plans.
	1. Blows up over trivial incidents.	
	2. Throws ball down in anger and performs badly after doing so.	
	3. Bad call by official causes poorer play.	
	4. Overdramatizes injury.	
	5. Complains.	
Self-confidence	**Confident**	Needs to be matched against a tough, confident competitor.
	1. Assertive in most situations.	
	2. Meets tough opponent "head on."	
	3. Comes out of game with head up, and he wants to go back.	
	4. Appears eager and anxious to compete.	
	Lacks Confidence	If possible, force him to make an error early in the game. It will badly disrupt him and he may never recover.
	1. Spends a lot of time watching other team.	
	2. Shy around other athletes.	
	3. Comes out of game with head down. Often appears beaten or depressed.	
Toughness	**Tough**	Prepare player to withstand rough treatment. He must be mentally tough in return.
	1. Undaunted by rough fans, verbal abuse by opponent, or bad calls by official.	
	2. Is openly defiant of opponent. Is often hostile toward the opponent. Sometimes refuses to shake hands.	

TABLE 5. (Continued)

Trait	Behavior Observed	Psychological Game Plan
Toughness (continued)	Tender 1. Shakes hand of opponent and is overly friendly. 2. Shies away from rough going in contest. 3. Withdraws and appears depressed after chewing out by coach.	Should receive rough treatment throughout the game. Attempt to intimidate and pressure early. Will have tendency to fail later.
Guilt Proneness	1. Walks with head down after doing poorly. Appears to be suffering for the whole team when things go wrong. 2. Throws up hands with air of futility.	If this player can be forced to make an error early in the game, he will rapidly become depressed, and his play will suffer as a result.
Exhibitionism	1. Wears some form of special gear or is particular about appearance. 2. Stays out on field longer than others. 3. Watches crowd (usually secretly). 4. Throws ball down; awaits crowd reaction.	Attempt to shut him out early so his need is not filled. He will begin to press and his effectiveness will diminish.
Anxiety	1. Keeps moving constantly. 2. Seeks encouragement from others. 3. Wipes hands continually.	Put pressure on this person early in game. Focus attention on him. Single him out and use his name.
Rigidity	1. Overanxious re plans and following rules. 2. Easily upset over broken plays. 3. Easily upset over broken rules or penalties. 4. Overconcerned about dress.	Force disruption of game plan. Rough up early —even commit obvious foul. Do everything to force him out of regular course of action.

General Observations About Coach

Observations	*Trait*
1. Does he watch the other team during warm-ups?	Anxiety Confidence
2. Does the coach often sit with his head down as if blaming himself for team errors?	Confidence
3. Does he pace?	Anxiety
4. Is he a yelling coach with his fist clenched? Are there any other signs of anger?	Aggression
5. Does he stay near or far from players during warm-ups and game?	Cohesion
6. Does he talk with sub-teams or individuals regularly during the game?	Cohesion
7. Does the coach disassociate himself during moments when the team is playing badly? When playing well?	Cohesion
8. Does the coach congratulate a player when he comes out of the game, or does he ignore him and walk away from him?	Cohesion

General Observations About Team

Observations	*Trait*
1. Do the players yell at officials?	Aggression Leadership
2. Are the pre-game drills well executed or are they somewhat chaotic and disorganized?	Discipline Organization
3. What is the general bench attitude? Enthusiastic? Indifferent? Unconcerned?	Cohesion
4. When behind, does the bench withdraw or does it get excited and more supportive?	Cohesion

General Observations About Team (Continued)

5. When team member does poorly, does the team   Cohesion
   support him, yell encouragement to him from the
   sidelines or from other positions on the field?

6. Notice players sitting next to coach and those far   Cohesion
   away from him. Are they always the same? (Those
   far away may be left out.)

logical strengths and weaknesses of his own team, the coach will learn how to prepare for an opponent. For example, if he learns to recognize and work with an unstable player on his own team, he will more readily recognize an unstable player on the other team.

Several methods may be used to get the required information:

Opponents evaluation card   The players are asked to evaluate their opponents along specific psychological lines on an opponent evaluation card. Essentially, the traits discussed in Chapter 3 are listed on a card and the individual players are asked to evaluate their opponent on a scale ranging from 1 to 5, with 1 being low and 5 being high. The player is then asked to make a brief statement concerning the opponent's major weakness and his major strength (see Figure 7).

The coach would also want to fill out an opponent evaluation card for each player and keep it with the others in his file. The same kind of a card should be made out by the coach on the team in general. The same traits would be evaluated along with the major strengths and weaknesses. The card should contain information on how many times the team was scouted and by whom.

Information derived outside the competitive situation Coaches love to talk to each other about their players, and quite often they describe characteristics that may give insight into the personality of those players. By making a mental note of what is said, the coach is provided with a guide for future observation.

FIGURE 7. Opponent Evaluation Card

Player: _____ Team: _____ Year: _____ Age: _____

Drive 1 2 3 4 5

Self-confidence 1 2 3 4 5

Intelligence 1 2 3 4 5   *Major Weaknesses:*

Aggressiveness 1 2 3 4 5

Determination 1 2 3 4 5

Emotional Stability 1 2 3 4 5

Response to Pressure 1 2 3 4 5

Leadership 1 2 3 4 5   *Major Strengths:*

Mental Toughness 1 2 3 4 5

Rapport with Teammates 1 2 3 4 5

Discipline 1 2 3 4 5

Endurance 1 2 3 4 5

Game: _____ Date: _____ Score: _____

The press may also give some insight into a situation that exists on a team or with an athlete. For example, an article may describe special team goals or even team problems. Because of the nature of his position, a sportswriter may be allowed to uncover information of a "personal" nature. The result may be a very detailed article which describes an individual athlete's goals, values, and even personal problems along with an analysis of his personality.

Player observations outside the competitive situation The players often have access to a great deal of information through their personal acquaintance with athletes on other teams. Word travels fast among the players and they can be an excellent source of information on opponents. The coach should routinely make out a player evaluation card immediately after receiving any information, because he may forget it and lose a possible advantage.

As a result of all the coach's efforts in the area of psychological scouting, he can prepare an opponent's file, containing a series of cards on individual players and teams.

PSYCHOLOGICAL GAME PLAN

After scouting for and acquiring the necessary information, the coach must integrate it into his game plan. The coach may have his team approach the opponent in two ways. Ordinarily he would concentrate on areas of weakness, but he may also attempt to meet and beat the opponent at his psychological strength. In the first instance, he would be using traits that are missing in opposing players or in the team as a whole. For example, an unaggressive tackle should have extremely aggressive play directed at him. A team that is not aggressive around the boards is probably susceptible to fierce, hard-nose tactics in that area. This is logical and basic to most coaches. In the other approach, however, the coach may choose to attack a team in its strongest area in an attempt to demoralize the team. It is, of course, a gamble, but one that can provide a big advantage if successful. To attack the opponent's strongest lineman and defeat him can crush a whole team. Outmuscling the other team's muscle-man establishes immediate supremacy. The latter approach symbolically defeats the team in general; the former approach focuses on the weakest individuals and defeats them one at a time. The most devastating approach is to use a combination of these two: attack the strength (if success is possible), while alternately picking on weaknesses throughout the rest of the squad.

In the psychological game plan, the coach should never have his players attempt too many things of a psychological nature against the opponent. It would become too complicated and disconcerting to the individuals attempting it. They will have enough to worry about, without being burdened by complex psychological information and tactics. Ideally, each player should concentrate on only one psychological weakness (or possibly two) in his opponent.

Quite obviously the coach will become aware of weaknesses on his own team. He must carefully prepare his players to meet the tactics that will be directed at them. He must stay with them and help them work through the problems, until they are confident that they can handle the attack. The coach will have some advantage here because he knows his own players much better than he knows the opponents, thus enabling him to start to work almost immediately on his own team's deficiencies.

Other psychological factors must be taken into account also. Players may be affected by the conditions under which they play. Poor lighting in a gym, fan-shaped backboards, small courts with close conditions, bare sections in the grass, wet areas, poor bench conditions, poor dressing facilities, rocky infields, unkept mounds, hard or soft tracks, etc. Younger players in particular may become greatly bothered by unfamiliar playing conditions. The coach should do what he can to prepare his players for all unusual situations in advance by discussing them with the players and then setting up similar conditions in the practice session.

The coach should openly discuss the opponent's psychological weaknesses with his team and provide a justification for using the tactics decided upon. The coach's approach to psychological game play should be direct and blunt, rather than scheming and conniving, to make it a legitimate and accepted part of a team's preparation for an opponent. With the information out in the open, the proper approach can be taken to prepare a player for competition.

SUMMARY

The main purpose of this book has been to acquaint the coach with those aspects of coaching for which he is rarely trained, but which often become the most difficult part of his job—

that of handling the interpersonal relations in athletics. A particular style of coaching has been advocated—that of considering the individual needs of each athlete and working toward helping each athlete attain those needs. To do this the coach must spend more time and effort with the individual athlete and must be more concerned with the motivational aspects of athletics, rather than techniques of play.

The coach should be forewarned that to apply this philosophy of coaching will require an adjustment period for him as well as for the team. As part of the philosophy, the coach may have to innovate and create new methods. This should be considered as part of his duties. Although the nature of athletics, as reflected in the rules and regulations, remains relatively stable, the nature of the coach's and athletes' personalities are always changing and dynamic. In order to deal with this, the coach must be flexible in his methods of handling each individual athlete.

When the coach uses all the information at his disposal —the psychological strengths and weaknesses of his players and their opponents, the outside influences affecting the athletes' attitudes, and the proper teaching, motivational, and communication techniques—and when he is able to determine not only the personal characteristics of his players, but also his own personality characteristics, he will be able to develop a positive philosophy of coaching. He can then decide the proper approach for preparing a player *completely* for athletic competition. This book is dedicated to that end.

INDEX

A

Adolescent, handling of, 63–66
Aggression, 43–44, 203
Analysis
  in information giving, 73
  of problem athletes, 77
Anger, 81–82
  negative, 82
  positive, 81
Anxiety, 206
Assessing personality traits, 47–49
Athlete
  his personality, 41–42
  handling "problems," 50–54
Athletic scope, 12
Athletic motivation inventory, 48–50
Attitude
  of the coach, 3
  problem areas, 181
Authoritarian coach (*see* "Hard-nosed" coach)

B

Behaviorial communication gaps, 95–96
"Business-like" coach, 35–39
  advantages, 37–38
  characteristics, 36–37
  disadvantages, 38–39

C

Coach
  personality, 16–17
  types, 15–39
  basis for respect, 10–12
Coach's attitude, 3–10
  approaching the athlete, 5–7
  competition and winning, 3–5
  losing, 9–10
  motivating the athlete, 7–9
Coachability, 44–45, 204
Coaching levels, 56–70
  adolescent, 63–66